D0394029

# How to Read a Person Like a Book

# How to Read a Person Like a Book

## by Gerard I. Nierenberg and Henry H. Calero

BARNES
&NOBLE
BOOKS
NEW YORK

C. 95
7.
6/00

This edition published by Barnes & Noble, Inc.,
by arrangement with the authors.

1994 Barnes & Noble Books

ISBN 1-56619-401-6

Printed and bound in the United States of America

M 9 8 7 6 5 4 3

**To Juliet and Barbara**

# Foreword

When this work was first published, it introduced a new discipline and a new awareness. The book has become the classic guide to interpreting body language. It is being used worldwide and has been translated into thirteen languages. *How To Read a Person Like a Book* presents a system for reading gestures that crosses all cultures and generations. Deciphering non-verbal communication opens the door to understanding what people are feeling, no matter what messages they may convey verbally. Every time you turn on the TV, you will recognize when a politician is trying to influence you, or when a salesman is making his pitch. Every time you go to a business meeting, you'll be able to recognize the prime players. If someone lies to you, you'll recognize the signs that cue you in to what's happening. You'll be sensitive to what's behind anger when it confronts you. In other words, you will be more finely tuned to the communication process, recognizing meanings and innuendoes that are not apparent in the spoken word. As a barometer of what people feel, gestures are more reliable than words.

In today's confused world, the insights provided by this book are now particularly relevant. We now recognize the importance of body language in communication. However, the structured guide to reading gestures contained herein is necessary.

- Male and female relationships are subject to misinterpretation, particularly since behavioral guidelines are unclear. Gesture reading is the important first step to building lasting relationships.
- We see politicians speak words that are geared to manipulate our thinking but we can recognize that the words do not match their non-verbal behavior.
- The media presents mixed visual and verbal messages to influence our decisions.
- We are continually inundated by sophisticated peddlers of misinformation who want our vote, our business, and our allegiance.

Fortune tellers now read their client's gestures as carefully as their palms. Even observant sales clerks recognize that shoppers who keep their hands deeply in their pockets are not buyers. Airline security officers now monitor the luggage check-in looking for people whose gestures make them suspicious. Bombings are aborted simply on the basis of accurately observing a passenger's gestures.

Can anyone doubt the importance of learning the intricacies of non-verbal behavior? Relying on the spoken word is not adequate. That's why *How To Read a Person Like a Book* is so essential a tool to better understanding between people. When this was written, I did not appreciate that it would be true in almost every situation and culture in the world.

Our function as human beings is to increase our expertise and to become so human that we see ourselves in all other people.

*Gerard I. Nierenberg*

# Contents

# How to Read a Person Like a Book

# CHAPTER 1

# Acquiring the Skills
# for Reading Gestures

"Learning is acquired by reading books,
but the much more necessary learning,
the knowledge of the world, is only to be
acquired by reading men, and studying
all the various editions of them."
—Lord Chesterfield, "Letters to His Son"

An airport is an excellent spot for viewing the entire human emotional spectrum. As travelers arrive and depart, you can see the woman who is very apprehensive about flying pinching the fleshy part of her hand for reassurance, as if she were saying to herself, "It's going to be all right." In the same manner people say, "I had to pinch myself to make sure that it wasn't a dream." A male waiting for departure time may also be unsure about flying. However, he is sitting in a rigid, upright position with his ankles locked. His hands are clenched together, making one big fist, while he rhythmically massages one thumb against the other on top of his interlocked hands. These gestures indicate a nervous attitude.

Walking away from the departure area, you see three men in telephone booths. One of them (Figure 1) is standing with his body at attention. His coat is buttoned. He gives the impression that whoever he is talking to is very important to him. He might be a salesman talking to a customer on the telephone as if he were actually in his presence.

The second caller's body is relaxed (Figure 2). He slouches over, shifts his weight from foot to foot, and rests his chin on his chest. He appears to be looking at the floor and nods his head as if saying, "Yeah, yeah." Reading this person further, you get the impression that he is comfortable but possibly bored with the conversation and attempting to hide the fact. The receiver of the call can be taken for granted. It is probably his wife or an old friend.

From these clues, can you visualize how a third caller might look as he talks to his girlfriend? This caller's face is hidden. His hunched shoulder may be concealing it from view or his body may be completely turned away from passers-by. His head is probably tilted to one side, and he handles the phone as if it were the object of his affection (Figure 3).

As you move toward the baggage-claim area, you may see a family group, which you can identify by the striking similarity in the way they all walk. Others on their way to the baggage-claim counter who have been met by family or friends usually appear the happiest and walk with a great deal of enthusiasm. Those who are waiting to be met keep rising on their toes and looking around.

During our brief visit to the airport we have become aware of the different actions of people. Merely by noting a variety of gestures we have been able to make guesses about people: attitudes, relationships, and situations. We have even conjured up an image of the person on the other end of the telephone line. Our observations have been of people acting and reacting in the real world, not in an isolated laboratory situation. In short, we have been exposed to the vast field of nonverbal communication that complements and supplements and can even displace verbal exchange. We have begun to read a person like a book.

. The salesman

2. The husband

3. The lover

3

## Life, the True Testing Ground

*"It's as large as life, and twice as natural!"*
*—Lewis Carroll, "Through the Looking Glass"*

Automobile manufacturers subject any new car accessory to extensive testing. However, it is not until the accessory is exposed to real-life situations that its success or failure can be definitively determined. Some years ago the Ford Motor Company decided to improve the safety of its automobile by adding an accessory called the vacuum automatic door lock, a device designed to lock the door automatically as soon as the car reached a speed of 9 m.p.h. After cars with the new locks were on the market, however, Ford began receiving complaint after complaint.

Whenever the buyers of these cars went to automatic car-washing stations they had trouble. As the automobile went down the washing line, the wheels were spun on the whitewall automatic washers and the car reached a relative speed of 9 m.p.h. The doors automatically locked, and at the end of the car-wash production line the drivers had to get a locksmith to pick the lock so they could get back into their own automobiles. So Ford went back to the drawing board and back to manually operated door locks.

In the same manner, life situations also offer better tests for the interpretation of gestures. The comprehension of gestures has not been achieved through the limited behavioral-laboratory approach, one which attempts to study individual parts abstracted from meaningful groups of gestures. It is a human process, and the methods that men have intuitively used for hundreds of thousands of years to understand one another naturally lend themselves as techniques for understanding gestures.

Our own awareness of nonverbal communications was an outgrowth of our interest in developing and teaching the art of negotiating. When we met and joined together to present workshops and seminars on negotiating to top executives in the United States and abroad, we were both aware of the vital role nonverbal communications play in every negotiating situation. We found that verbal exchange does not operate in a vacuum; rather, it is a complex process involving people, words, and body movements. It was only by considering these elements together that we could follow the progress of a negotiation.

We found that one limiting factor to studying gestures has been the lack of a simple system of transcribing or reproducing an actual situation where individuals could be thoroughly observed and the interaction or expressive behavior between subjects studied systematically. With the video-tape recorder we were able to eliminate this first difficulty.

Ray Birdwhistell, senior research scientist at Eastern Pennsylvania Research Institute, is presently engaged in filming encounters and noting them through kinesics, a science that sets out to analyze individual gestures by considering their component parts. This book considers the problem of nonverbal communication in a different manner. We have considered Norbert Wiener's admonition in *Cybernetics*: "Many a missionary has fixed his own misunderstanding of a primitive language as law eternal in the process of reducing it to writing. There is much in the social habits of a people which is dispersed and distorted by the mere act of making inquiries about it." In addition to viewing individual gestures we present the myriad of attitudes expressed by not one gesture but a series of related ones. These we call gesture-clusters. They are groups of nonverbal communications associated with different attitudes. The gestures that comprise a cluster can occur at the same time, as locking arms and ankles and making a fist, or occur one after the other. In video-tape recording we have a useful tool for capturing and preserving these gesture-clusters, and the seminar participants' role-playing for gesture-analysis in negotiating situations have provided us with our raw material.

We have held hundreds of seminars with thousands of participants and have recorded 2,500 negotiating situations. Our audiences have not only provided the research material on gestures but also acted as the researchers. We presented the gestures to them individually and in video-taped clusters and then asked our seminar audiences what they recognized, what the feeling or message of the nonverbal communication was. We first merely wanted the audience to recognize the gestures by separating them from nonmeaningful body movements. We then wanted the audience to give gestures their meaning.

As a result of many discussions it came to our attention that when the audiences began to recognize the meaning of certain gestures, they more or less relied upon getting the meaning by a subconscious empathy. That is, the viewer would empathize with the observed, empathize with his body tensions and positions, and understand the gesture's meaning by putting himself in the place of the person he was viewing. However, when gestures are merely read subconsciously, only unconscious assumptions about them can be made. Sigmund Freud wrote, "The unconscious of one human being can react upon that of another without passing through the conscious." These unconscious reactions then become untested "facts" to which we respond. If we subconsciously conceive of the gesture as unfriendly, without conscious control we bring about a belligerent reaction that degenerates into a vicious cycle of hostility. As thinking men, we should be able to evaluate most stimuli before reacting to them.

If we could stop and read gestures consciously, if we could subject them to examination and verification, it is possible that before communications degenerate we could elevate the process to a different plane. We might read our own gestures and find that we are precipitating the other person's reactions.

Or the gestures that we find undesirable might be found to be merely the result of the other person's physical idiosyncrasies. For example, a certain judge grimaced and blinked at lawyers appearing before him, causing considerable alarm among those inclined to be self-conscious or nervous. The judge suffered from the results of a stroke that left him with gestural scars. There are also misunderstandings because the same gesture can produce completely different responses in different cultures. Still other gestures may be repeated merely because of habit and do not signal a currently held attitude, whatever their origin. Gestures, then, appear to be made more meaningful by being brought out of the subconscious and recognized on the conscious level. We can term this *thinking through to the subconscious*. In this way we get a message rather than just a subconscious empathetic feeling.

## Gestures Come in Clusters

"His nose should pant and his lip should curl,
His cheek should flame and his brow should furl,
His bosom should heave and his heart should
    glow,
And his fist be ever ready for a knock-down
    blow."
—W. S. Gilbert, "H.M.S. Pinafore"

The understanding of gestures is very difficult when the various elements are separated from their context. However, when gestures are fitted together into their composite positions, a complete picture evolves.

Each gesture is like a word in a language. In order to be understood in a language, one must structure his words into units, or "sentences," that express complete thoughts. It is not unusual for attendees at our seminars to attempt to bridge this word/sentence gap quickly. Some sincerely believe that a cursory exposure to the world of nonverbal communication equips them to speak the "language" fluently. On the contrary, this serves only to bring their awareness to a conscious level, not to make them experts. We attempt to discourage individuals from jumping to immediate conclusions based on the observation and comprehension of isolated gestures. Understanding the congruence of gestures in harmony with one another is far more important. A static gesture lasting several seconds might be contradicted by a prior body movement (incongruence), which in turn might be further repudiated by a subsequent gesture.

The so-called nervous laugh is a good example of incongruity. In every instance that we have recorded of the nervous laugh there has been an incongruity between the sound, which should indicate amusement, and the rest of the gesture-cluster, which signals extreme discomfort. Not only are there nervous arm and leg movements, but the entire body shifts as though trying to escape from an unpleasant situation. This gesture-cluster seldom results from a humorous statement. It indicates that the laugher is unsure of himself or even somewhat frightened by a situation.

By mentally matching congruent gestures that form clusters we can understand the attitudes expressed and discover some meaning. Indeed, what we should look for are similar attitudinal gestures that not only endorse one another but serve to make a cluster. As an example, a congruent set of gestures for a salesman who is very anxious and enthusiastic about his product might be sitting on the edge of his chair, feet apart, possibly on the toes in a sprinter's position, hand on the table, body leaning forward. Facial congruence might amplify the posture: eyes alert, a slight smile, and, probably, no furrow on the brow.

Understanding congruency of gestures serves as a monitoring device for discovering a person's attitude and then giving his actions meaning. It serves as an "anti-assumption" control that forces us to observe further before jumping to a conclusion. Initially, it appears very easy to read individual gestures and have fun determining what they may mean. However, the serious student of gestures soon understands that each gesture can quickly be countered, amplified, and confused by another. At various times, people without nonverbal-communication-awareness training have probably made quick judgments concerning gestural meaning without considering congruency. From our experience these were the instances that proved most disastrous to them.

One of our fellow researchers in England, Dr. D. A. Humphries, asked us about the reliability of nonverbal elements in verbal exchanges. We mentioned that in our early research we sometimes found a dichotomy between obvious verbal and nonverbal meanings. It was only after a later, fuller evaluation of the situations that we found that the nonverbal gesture proved to be the more truthful. So the congruence of gestures not only concerns us with matching gesture with gesture but with verbal/gesture evaluation. It is the gesture-endorsing spoken word that is important for total communication. Politicians can win or lose campaigns depending on whether they maintain congruence. Now that television plays such a prominent part in political campaigns, the congruence of gesticulation becomes extremely important in presenting arguments. Unfortunately, however, we still can see many a high-ranking politician using gestures that are incongruent with his speech. While saying, "I'm sincerely receptive to a dialogue with the young people," for example, he shakes his finger and then his fist at his audience. Or he attempts to convince his audience of his warm, humane approach while using short, violent karate hand chops at the lectern.

Here is a test to determine how congruence can assist you.

The following passage from Charles Dickens's *Great Expectations* is a scene for the reader to visualize:

> Casting my eyes along the street at a certain point of my progress, I beheld Trabb's boy approaching, lashing himself with an empty blue bag. Deeming that a serene and unconscious contemplation of him would best beseem me, and would be most likely to quell his evil mind, I advanced with that expression of countenance, and was rather congratulating myself on my success, when suddenly the knees of Trabb's boy smote together, his hair uprose, his cap fell off, he trembled violently in every limb, staggered out into the road, and crying to the populace, "Hold me! I'm so frightened!" feigned to be in a paroxysm of terror and contrition, occasioned by the dignity of my appearance. As I passed him, his teeth loudly chattered in his head, and with every mark of extreme humiliation, he prostrated himself in the dust.

After having read this passage, attempt, without rereading, to visualize the people and the scene. Picture in your mind's eye what the writer described and then write down what you saw. Then reread the paragraph to see how accurately you remembered it. Now see if you can remember more. Having in mind a congruence of gestures that the author is very much aware of, try the same visualization experiment with the next paragraph, but tie the gestures together, forming a memory chain:

> This was a hard thing to bear, but this was nothing. I had not advanced another two hundred yards, when to my inexpressible terror, amazement, and indignation, I again beheld Trabb's boy approaching. He was coming round a narrow corner. His blue bag was slung over his shoulder, honest industry beamed in his eyes, a determination to

proceed to Trabb's with cheerful briskness was indicated in his gait. With a shock he became aware of me, and was severely visited as before; but this time his motion was rotatory, and he staggered round and round me with knees more afflicted, and with up-lifted hands as if beseeching for mercy. His sufferings were hailed with the greatest joy by a knot of spectators, and I felt utterly confounded.

Congruence can provide a structure on which human actions can be ordered and thereby recalled more easily. The problem with observing congruence is that we tend to "tune in and out" not only verbal communication but also nonverbal messages. As an example, imagine an individual briskly walking into your office. He says good morning, unbuttons his coat, sits down with his body relaxed, legs spread apart, slight smile on his face, hands lightly resting on the arms of the chair. Thus far, all congruent gestures indicate that the person is receptive, open, not defensive, and probably at ease or comfortable with the environment. Once having organized the initial gestures into a composite attitude or feeling, you will find it easy to turn off your visual reception in favor of the audio and relax into a complacent belief that everything is going well. The rude awakening comes when you are jarred from your lethargy by an awareness that something has gone wrong. The person is now talking with his fists clenched, or he is shaking his index finger at you. In addition to scowling, he is getting red in the face either from heat or anger. The environment has quickly deteriorated into a rather sticky situation from which you must either extricate yourself or face a hostile friend, client, or customer.

Although at first it is difficult to concentrate on seeing gestures objectively, by exercising our awareness daily it becomes much easier, as in learning any language. And as for congruity, if instead of concentrating on gestures as mere parts that must be fitted together for meaning we concentrate upon the gesture-clusters, then congruity of body movements and gestures becomes considerably simpler to understand. This contributes greatly to *seeing* the overall meaning.

## How You Can Benefit by Understanding Gestures

**"Watch out for the man whose stomach doesn't move when he laughs."**
                            **—Cantonese proverb**

People can communicate different types of information at different levels of understanding. The communication process consists of more than the spoken or written language. When you are trying to communicate with a person, sometimes you get through and sometimes you do not—not because of what you said or how you said it or the logic of your thoughts, but because many times the reception of your communication is based upon the degree of the listener's empathy for your nonverbal communication. A husband turning his back on his wife and slamming the front door without a word is heralding a significant message. It is therefore not very difficult to understand what benefits a person can derive from understanding nonverbal language, since we communicate in a multiprocess manner. Keep in mind, however, that your emotional relations, mannerisms, habits, and gestures are separate and distinct from those of the person sitting next to you at a business conference or party, at a ballgame or bar, or on the subway or bus. Also, dealing with people by lumping them into one category or another has more dangers than rewards.

Observing and becoming aware of gestures is fairly simple, but interpreting them is something else. As an example, we have recorded, observed, and had corroborated by other researchers the gesture of covering one's mouth while speaking.

There is agreement that this is an indication that one is unsure of what he is saying. If you then find yourself listening to an individual who suddenly starts to speak through his hands, is he lying? unsure? doubting what he is saying? Possibly any of these. But before you jump to a conclusion, recall (if you can) whether the person has previously spoken in that manner. What were the circumstances? If not, consider that he may have had some recent dental work that might cause him to become self-conscious when talking, or that someone may have told him he has bad breath. If he has a track record of covering his mouth while speaking, continue to Phase II of the analysis. After he says something that you would like to test, ask him, "Are you sure?" Such a direct question can be answered with a simple yes. It can also make him very defensive, in which case you will know that he is not sure of what he has said. Or he will react to your question by saying something like, "Now that you mention it, I guess I'm really not sure." As with verbal understanding, we must consider more than the individual unit out of context. Experience, alternative verification, and congruency are important ingredients. However, in situations where one cannot use the usual methods of confirmation, consideration should be given to a consensus on the meaning of the hand-over-mouth gesture: The many law-enforcement people who have attended our seminars state without exception that the gesture indicates that the person is doubtful, unsure, lying, or distorting the truth.

One of the participants in our seminar, in discussing non-verbal communication, reported the following: "On returning from the Chicago seminar I was seated next to a woman who explained that she was a registered nurse. She then proceeded to tell me all that was wrong with the medical profession. From my point of view she was overgeneralizing and drew conclusions that I believed to be false. The point of all this is that while I was attempting to listen I had my arms folded high on my chest, feeling very stubbornly that she didn't know what she was talking about. When I discovered myself in this position, I understood what was taking place within me. I tried a different approach. I uncrossed my arms and proceeded to listen without evaluating. As a result I was able to listen more intently. I became less defensive and was able to realize that although I disagreed, she was saying something I was now able to listen to more fully and appreciate."

The folded-arms gesture can be understood and utilized in another way: While trying to communicate with someone, we may notice him taking this position like some bygone cigar-store Indian. This is one of the gestures that indicate he is not going to listen and is very adamant about it. In many conversations, rather than recognizing this and coping with it by trying alternative methods and courses open to us, we proceed in the same conversational pattern and talk a blue streak. Therefore, instead of helping the individual to cooperate in the communication, we tend to drive him further away.

Feedback plays a major role in the full communication process, and gesture-clusters are an important feedback. They indicate from moment to moment and movement to movement exactly how individuals or groups are reacting nonverbally. We can learn whether what we are saying is being received in a positive manner or a negative one, whether the audience is open or defensive, self-controlled or bored. Speakers call this audience-awareness, or relating to a group. Nonverbal feedback can warn you that you must change, withdraw, or do something different in order to bring about the result that you desire. If you are *not* aware of feedback, then there is a strong possibility that you will fail to communicate your believ-ability or sincerity to an individual or to an audience.

An attorney who attended one of our seminars sent us a letter in which he explained the benefits he had derived from consciously considering nonverbal communication. He said in the course of an office visit his client crossed his arms and legs "in a defensive position" and proceeded to spend the next hour admonishing him. Noticing the nonverbal implications of the client's gestures, he let his client talk it out of his system. Only after this did the lawyer offer professional advice on how to handle the difficult situation the client found himself in. The attorney stated that had he not attended our seminar he would not have given his client a chance to be receptive to him, since he would not have read his client's needs and would probably have attempted immediately to give him unheeded advice.

A common observation seminar attendees make is, "I feel frustrated because despite the fact that I'm aware that gestures exist, I find myself tuned out for periods of as long as fifteen minutes where I'm absolutely unaware of what's going on." The art of thoroughly seeing nonverbal communications is a learning process almost as difficult as acquiring fluency in a foreign language. In addition to maintaining a conscious awareness of your own gestures and the meaning you are conveying to your audience, we recommend that you set aside at least ten minutes a day during which you consciously "read" the gestures of others. Anywhere that people gather is an excellent "reading" ground. Social and business gatherings that permit freely expressed emotions and the possibility of polarization of attitudes are especially well-suited for doing thorough research. The attitudes of people attending these functions are usually so intense that each tends to be "wearing his feelings on his sleeve." However, you do not have to leave your home to do homework. Television offers a fertile field for reading nonverbal communication, particularly the interview and discussion programs. Try to understand what is happening by just watching the picture. Turn on the sound at five-minute intervals to check the verbal communication against your reading of the gestures. Be sure to watch for congruency and gesture-clusters.

# CHAPTER 2

# Materials
# for Gesture-Reading

" 'Tis the sublime of man . . . to know
ourselves parts and proportions of one
wondrous whole!"
—Samuel Taylor Coleridge, "Religious Musings"

A storehouse of information on the observation of gestures and
their interpretive meanings has been made available to us
every time we have conducted a seminar. We usually devote
the initial segment of the seminar to asking people to comment
on gestures that they have observed and to consider possible
meanings. Some of the more obvious gestures, such as folded
arms, are quickly associated with a defensive posture. However, some—such as steepling (putting the fingertips together)
(see Figure 40)—are often misinterpreted as something other
than confidence. When we discuss the data gathered on this
gesture and ask how a person might react in a real-life situation to someone who steeples, the majority agrees that a confident attitude and the steepling gesture are indeed congruous.
Add to this gesture a slight turning up of the lips in a faint
smile and most will accept the label "the cat that swallowed
the canary" gesture.

The individual significance of a gesture is sometimes subject to as many interpretations as the number of persons evaluating it. But we must remember that each gesture is only one input and that the total congruent communication picture is what we are seeking. We should not be completely influenced by observing only one signal and making a decision while being unaware of the gesture-cluster and the prior and subsequent gestures.

In order to comprehend the full meaning of a gesture-cluster and determine the congruity of its components, let us first look at several types of nonverbal communication that are easily recognizable and often encountered.

## Facial Expressions

> "The eyes of men converse as much as
> their tongues, with the advantage that the
> ocular dialect needs no dictionary, but is
> understood the world over."
> —Ralph Waldo Emerson

Easily the least controversial of all the areas of nonverbal communication is facial expression, as this is the most readily observed group of gestures. We focus our eyes on the face more often than on any other part of the body, and the expressions we see there have widely accepted meanings. At some time or another almost everyone has encountered "a look that could kill," "a fish eye," a "come-hither look," or an "I'm available" glance.

During a business negotiation one can observe a wide range of facial expressions: At one extreme is the aggressively hostile negotiator who sees a negotiation as an arena where a "do or die" situation exists; he typically looks at you with eyes wide open, lips tightly closed, and corners of his eyebrows down, and sometimes he even talks through his teeth with very little movement of lips. At the other end of the spectrum is the individual who approaches the negotiation table with impeccable manners and a choirboy look of half-closed or somewhat droopy eyelids, a veiled, slight smile, and peacefully arched eyebrows without any furrow on the forehead. However, he is probably a very capable and competitive individual who believes in cooperation as a dynamic process.

Jane Templeton, a psychologist who recently wrote an article for *Marketing Magazine* entitled "How Salesmen Can Find Out What's Really on a Customer's Mind," observed:

> If a prospect's eyes are downcast and face turned away, you're being shut out. However, if the mouth is relaxed, without the mechanical smile, chin is forward, he is probably considering your presentation. If his eyes engage yours for several seconds at a time with a slight, one-sided smile extending at least to nose level, he is weighing your proposal. Then if his head is shifted to the same level as yours, smile is relaxed and appears enthusiastic, the sale is virtually made.

We have discovered that many persons who acknowledge that communication through facial expression exists have never attempted to understand specifically how they communicate. For example, any poker player clearly understands what you mean when you say that he has a "poker face." However, very few of them actually attempt to analyze the underlying meaning—expressing no emotions, blank look, zero disclosure, stoic expression, etc.

One of the initial methods we use to help establish aware-

ness in our seminars is a visual-aid slide showing two groups sitting on opposite sides of a conference table (Figure 4). It is evident from the facial expressions that those sitting on the right side are contented, confident, and smug, and those on the left are unhappy, angry, and defensive.

After viewing this on a large screen, the attendees agree that the groups appear to be divided into two opposing camps. Once we have obtained this concession, we ask, "In what way is this communicated to you?" Although some never say more than "facial expressions," others, with more perception, note in detail the furrows of the forehead, eyebrow positioning, exaggerated opening of the eyes, flaring nostrils, and so on.

**4. Opposing camps**

Charles Darwin in his classic book, *The Expression of Emotion in Man and Animals*, to ascertain "whether the same expressions and gestures prevail . . . with all the races of mankind," wrote questions to his correspondents scattered throughout the world. As simple as the questions were, he requested that even his trained observers use "actual observations, and not memory." The following are a few of Darwin's questions:

1. Is astonishment expressed by the eyes and mouth being opened wide, and by the eyebrows being raised?
2. Does shame excite a blush when the colour of the skin

allows it to be visible? And especially how low down the body does the blush extend?

3. When a man is indignant or defiant does he frown, hold his body and head erect, square his shoulders and clench his fists?

4. When considering deeply on any subject, or trying to understand any puzzle, does he frown, or wrinkle the skin beneath the lower eyelids?

To these and other basic questions he received replies from thirty-six different observers in various parts of the world. Their answers showed a great deal of similarity in communication through facial expressions.

A British research team led by Christopher Brannigan and David Humphries isolated and catalogued 135 distinct gestures and expressions of face, head, and body. Of these, 80 were involved in face and head gestures. They recorded nine separate smiles, three of which are very common: simple smile, upper smile, and broad smile. Briefly analyzed, the *simple smile* (Figure 5A), with teeth unexposed, is commonly seen when a person is not participating in any outgoing activity. He is smiling to himself. In the *upper smile* (Figure 5B) the upper incisors are exposed and there is usually eye-to-eye contact between the individuals. It is often used as a greeting smile when friends meet, or, sometimes, when children greet their parents. A *broad smile* (Figure 5C) is commonly seen during play and is often associated with laughing; both upper and lower incisors are exposed, and eye-to-eye contact seldom occurs.

Smiles should not always be associated strictly with happy moments. "Beware of the oblong smile," says Dr. Ewan Grant of Birmingham University. He uses this name for the smile that many of us tend to use when we have to be polite. The lips are drawn fully back from both upper and lower teeth, forming the oblong with the lips. Somehow there is no depth

**5A. Simple smile**

**5B. Upper smile**

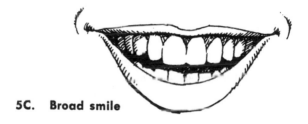

**5C. Broad smile**

to this smile. "This is the smile or grimace when one is pretending to enjoy a joke or off-the-cuff remark. Or when a girl gets too much attention from a drunk, or is being chased around the office by the boss."

The oblong smile is one of the five basic smiles that Grant has defined. Another is the upper, or how-do-you-do, smile, in which only the upper teeth are uncovered and the mouth generally is only slightly open. The simple smile, a "typically nonsense smile," occurs when someone is by himself and happy. The lips curve back and up but remain together, so there is no dental display. The broad smile occurs "in situations of pleasurable excitement": The mouth is open, the lips curled right back, and both upper and lower teeth can be seen. The lip-in smile is often seen on the faces of coy girls. It is much the same as the upper smile except that the lower lip is drawn in between the teeth. "It implies that the person feels in some way subordinate to the person she is meeting."

Conflict between individuals brings forth very different expressions. Eyebrows are usually down, particularly at the inner ends, producing a frown. At the same time, the lips are tensed and pushed slightly forward, though teeth are not shown. The head, and often the chin, is thrust forward in a very defiant move, and the eyes glare at the adversary in an "eyeball-to-eyeball" confrontation. In situations such as this, both individuals rarely lose eye contact with each other, since this would signal defeat or fear by the person looking away. Instead, the eyes seem to be staring hypnotically and concentration is intense.

Facial expressions can also express shock or great surprise. In these emotional states a person's mouth is wide open because the jaw muscles are relaxed due to shock and the chin drops. There is, however, a time when the mouth unconsciously opens and it is not due to shock or surprise. This happens when a person concentrates on one thing so intently— for example, when attempting to fit together delicate parts of a mechanism—that every muscle in his face below the eyes is completely relaxed. Sometimes the tongue even protrudes from the mouth.

Many of us, no doubt, have reached the conclusion that people who do not look at us while either listening or talking are trying to hide something. This is in general agreement with the opinion of law-enforcement officials who have attended our seminars. Michael Argyle in his book, *The Psychology of Interpersonal Behavior,* observes that people look at each other between 30 and 60 percent of the time. He also notes that when two individuals while talking look at each other more than 60 percent of the time, they probably are more interested in the other person than in what he is saying. Two extremes might be lovers looking at each other adoringly and two hostile individuals getting ready to fight. Argyle also believes that abstract thinkers tend to have more eye contact than those who think in concrete terms, because abstract thinkers have a greater ability to integrate incoming data and are less likely to be distracted by eye contact.

We have also found that people tend to have eye contact more when they listen than when talking. They also employ a gaze aversion when asked questions that make them feel uncomfortable or guilty. On the other hand, when asked a question or when reacting to a statement that makes them feel defensive, aggressive, or hostile, their eye contact increases dramatically. You can sometimes clearly see the pupils dilate when a person is thus aroused.

As with every rule, there are exceptions. The amount of eye contact varies dramatically with different individuals and cultures. Certain individuals, due to their shyness, tend to avoid eye contact or at least minimize it if at all possible. These persons could possibly be the most honest, sincere, and dedicated individuals around. However, every time they fail to look at the other person, they are unintentionally communicating doubt and possible prevarication. If you have gone through U.S. Customs, you may recall that when you approached the agent, in spite of the fact that you had given him a filled-out declaration form, he asked if you had anything to declare. Do you remember if he looked at the form or into your eyes? Chances are that he looked you right in the eye even though he had the declaration form in hand. As Jean de la Fontaine said, "It is a double pleasure to deceive the deceiver."

"Giving someone the eye" describes a facial expression with eye contact that indicates interest, however brief the glance may be. The *paseo* in Latin-American countries is a ritual devoted almost exclusively to this form of nonverbal communication. Each Sunday unattached young men and women gather in the town square. The eligible men walk in one direction and the women in the other. If any of them is given the eye and the interest seems to be reciprocated, on the next trip around, a few words may be exchanged, and this may lead to a date.

The sidelong glance is known in both Spanish and English

as the stolen look. It is used by secretive persons who want to see but not be caught at it. At the other extreme is the glance under lowered eyelids. The lids are lowered not to hide the eyes but to concentrate the glance on an interesting object. Painters looking at work in progress and lovers offering undying devotion are especially prone to it.

George Porter, who has written a series of articles on nonverbal communication for the *Training and Development Journal,* notes that displeasure or confusion may be shown by a frown; envy or disbelief might be displayed by a raised eyebrow; and antagonism shown through the tightening of the jaw muscles or by the squinting of the eyes. In addition there is the quite common gesture of thrusting out the chin as a defiant little boy might do when rebelling against his parents. Also, when a person's jaw muscles tighten as he becomes antagonistic, watch his lips. They too tighten in a pursing gesture. The pursing action communicates that he has taken a defensive position and will reveal or react as little as possible. This possibly gave rise to the expression "tight-lipped."

## Walking Gestures

"Awkward, embarrassed, stiff, without the skill
Of moving gracefully or standing still,
One leg, as if suspicious of his brother,
Desirous seems to run away from t'other."
—Charles Churchill, "The Rosciad"

Everyone has a distinctive walk that makes him easily recognizable to his friends. Certain characteristics are due at least in part to body structure, but pace, length of stride, and posture seem to change with the emotions. If a child is happy, he moves more quickly and is very light on his feet. If not, his shoulders droop, and he walks as though the soles of his shoes were made of lead. The young cock of the walk is well-described by Shakespeare in *Troilus and Cressida:* "A strutting player whose conceit lies in his hamstring." Generally, adults who walk rapidly and swing their arms freely tend to be goal-oriented and readily pursue their objectives, while the person who habitually walks with his hands in his pockets, even in warm weather, tends to be critical and secretive. He generally plays the role of devil's advocate quite well, since he likes to put other people down.

When people are dejected they scuffle along with their hands in their pockets, seldom looking up or noticing where they are headed. It is not unusual to see a person in this frame of mind walking near the curb with his eyes staring at whatever might be lying in it (Figure 6). There is a story of a priest who,

**6. The dejected walker**

**7. The burst-of-energy walker**

spotting such an individual one morning and taking pity on him, handed him two dollars with a consoling "Never despair." The following morning the priest again saw the same man, who this time came up to him, handed him forty dollars, and said, "Never Despair won and paid twenty to one."

The person who walks with hands on hips (Figure 7) is more like a sprinter than a long-distance runner. He wants to go the shortest possible distance in the fastest possible time to reach his goal. His sudden bursts of energy are often followed by periods of seeming lethargy while he plans his next decisive move. Perhaps the most famous walker of this type was Sir Winston Churchill. The stance was as characteristic of him as his "V for Victory" sign.

People who are preoccupied with a problem will often assume a meditative pose while walking: head down, hands clasped behind their back (Figure 8). Their pace is very slow and they may pause to kick over a rock or even reach down to

8. **The preoccupied walker**

9. **The strutter**

turn over a scrap of paper and leave it on the ground. They seem to be saying to themselves, "Let's look at this from all sides."

The self-satisfied, somewhat pompous person may signal his state of mind with a walk that Benito Mussolini made famous (Figure 9). His chin is raised, the arms have an exaggerated swing, the legs are somewhat stiff, and the pace is deliberate, calculated to impress.

"Setting the pace" is an expression that applies equally well to leaders of men whose subordinates keep in step behind them and to formations of ducklings following their mother. It is a sign of the followers' loyalty and devotion. In every society the leaders set the pace. This simple observation has provided Kremlinologists with thousands of words of copy about the Soviet leadership and the F.B.I. with valuable information about who is who in the Mafia. It can also help you if you prefer to deal with the top man in any organization.

## Shaking Hands

> "There is a hand that has not heart in it,
> there is a claw or paw, a flipper or fin, a
> bit of wet cloth to take hold of, a piece of
> unbaked dough, a cold clammy thing we
> recoil from, or greedy clutch with the heat
> of sin, which we drop as a burning coal."
> —C. A. Bartol, "The Rising Faith"

Many a male can recall a close relative saying to him, "I'm going to teach you how to shake hands like a man." There followed instructions on how to grip the other person's hand, how to squeeze it firmly, and how to release it. But no one teaches a businesswoman how to shake hands "like a woman." She develops a firm handshake out of self-defense, having constantly encountered businessmen who automatically extend their hand in greeting "like a man."

Women, when expressing sincere feelings to other women, particularly during a crisis, do not shake hands. They gently hold the other's hands in theirs and with congruous facial expressions communicate their deep sympathy (Figure 10). Often an embrace that endorses their attitude will follow. Very seldom will a woman use this gesture with a man. It seems to be specially reserved for communication with her own sex.

A handshake is a modification of the primitive gesture of both hands raised, indicating that no weapons are held. Later the greeting was the Roman salute, a hand-to-chest gesture. During the time of the Roman Empire, men grasped each other at the forearms instead of the hand. The modern handshake is a gesture of welcome: the palms interlocking signify openness and the touching signifies oneness.

Handshaking customs vary from country to country. The French shake hands on entering and leaving a room. The Germans pump hands one time only. Some Africans snap their fingers after each handshake to signify freedom; still others

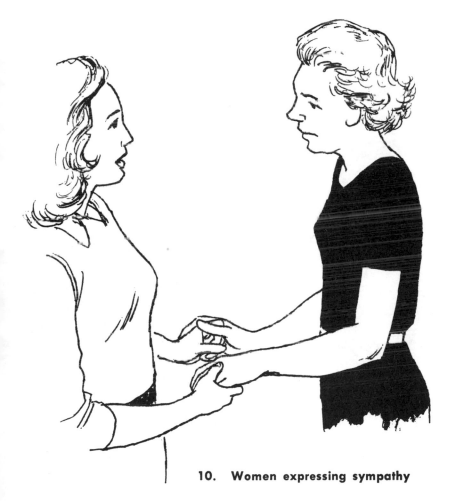

**10.  Women expressing sympathy**

**11.   The politician's handshake**

consider handshaking in bad taste. Whatever the situation, find out the local custom before making the assumption that your brand of handshake will be acceptable. The firmness of the typical male handshake in the United States probably originated in contests of strength, such as Indian wrestling.

Many people consider themselves experts in analyzing character and attitude from a handshake. In almost universal disfavor is the clammy handshake, probably because perspiring palms usually indicate nervousness. The flaccid, or "dead fish," handshake is equally unpopular, although here there may be mitigating circumstances. Many athletes are overly cautious about controlling their strength when shaking hands and, as a result, use very little pressure. Skilled artists, such as musicians and surgeons, are very concerned with their hands and will take defensive measures to protect them. But in the United States at least there is something vaguely un-American about a flaccid handshake.

Typically American is what we term the politician's handshake. During election campaigns it is used by candidates for offices ranging from dogcatcher to President. The usual form is to grasp a hand with the right and cup it with the left hand (Figure 11). Almost as popular is shaking with the right while grasping the other person's right forearm or right shoulder with the left hand. For two dear friends to greet in this manner is acceptable, but most people feel very uncomfortable when someone whom they do not know intimately shakes hands with them in this manner. They tend to see the gesture as insincere and falsely ingratiating, yet many politicians persist in using it.

It is difficult for some people without in-depth exposure to nonverbal communications not to jump to immediate conclusions about others by only seeing their facial expressions or the way they walk or shake hands. Reserve your judgments. See how much more you can learn by knowing attitudes and gesture-clusters.

# CHAPTER 3

# Openness, Defensiveness, Evaluation, Suspicion

"My clothes keep my various selves
buttoned up together, and enable all these
otherwise irreconcilable aggregates of
psychological phenomena to pass
themselves off as one person."
—Logan Pearsall Smith, "More Trivia"

Now that we have examined a few individual gestures, we will consider attitudes and their gesture-clusters. We have tried wherever possible to arrange attitudes in contrasting pairs, openness and defensiveness, evaluation and suspicion, and so forth. It is rarely possible to see all the gestures that make up a cluster. Just a few observations, however, can give you an idea of what attitude the other person has at the moment. By seeing the attitudes contrasted you can also appreciate any emotional movement and its direction, for example, changing from openness to defensiveness. Also, because there are many overlapping attitudinal positions, we have grouped them so that every second attitude is similar to the one in the preceding pair to show their similarities and differences, as in defensiveness and suspicion, readiness and cooperation, and confidence and self-control.

With very few exceptions, people nonverbally communicate their inner feelings quite openly. If their verbal statements are consistent with emotions and attitudes revealed through gestures, they are probably telling the truth. Look for consistency between the verbal and the nonverbal communication, and congruence between individual gestures and gesture-clusters. The ability to do so will serve you very well in everyday judgments of your business and social contacts.

## Openness

> "The young man, who intends no ill,
> believes that none is intended, and therefore
> acts with openness and candor; but his
> father, having suffered the injuries of fraud,
> is impelled to suspect, and too often
> allured to practice it."
> —Samuel Johnson, "Rasselas"

Once people have been exposed to the idea of attempting to read through to the subconscious by closely observing gestures, the question they are most likely to ask is, "How can I tell when someone is lying?" The television program *To Tell the Truth* can serve as a laboratory for testing your ability to apply your awareness of gestures to separate truth-tellers from liars. The program presents groups of three people who are questioned by a panel. Two of them will lie and attempt to conceal their true identity; one tells the truth. Observing their stance, facial expressions, and other body gestures, and matching these with what they say can strengthen your ability to pick out those who prevaricate.

Those gestures and gesture-clusters used by the falsifiers which indicate secretiveness, defensiveness, or concealment are discussed in later sections. Distinguishing these from openness gestures will help you recognize the untruthful person.

**12. Open hands
signaling sincerity**          **13. "What do you want me to do?"**

There are many gestures that are parts of openness clusters.
Among these are:

Open Hands (Figure 12). One gesture that most of us
readily associate with sincerity and openness is open hands.
Italians use the open-hands gesture freely. When they are
overtly frustrated they lay their open hands on their chest
and gesture, "What do you want me to do?" The shoulder-
shrugging gesture is also accompanied by open hands, palms
upward (Figure 13). Actors use this gesture in many expressive ways, not only to show emotion but to indicate the open
nature of the character even before the actor speaks. Watch
children when they are proud of what they have accomplished.
They show their hands openly. But when they feel guilty or
suspicious about a situation, they hide their hands either in
their pockets or behind their back.

Unbuttoning Coat. Men who are open or friendly toward you frequently unbutton their coats or even take them off in your presence. David Frost, on his television interview program, regularly unbuttons his coat when greeting a guest. We were told at our seminar in Jamaica, "Here, at a business conference, when people start taking off their coats, you know that they are communicating that some sort of agreement is possible. Regardless of the heat, a businessman will not remove his coat when he feels no settlement or agreement is near."

As with other attitudes, openness encourages similar feelings in others. Charles Darwin noted this interaction when he wrote that he frequently observed animals communicating submissiveness, a form of openness, when they lay on their backs and exposed their soft underparts and throats to their opponents. He noted that in such situations even the most hostile animal did not take advantage of the vanquished. In a recent article, Dr. Leon Smith, a comparative psychologist who specializes in the learning and communication process of animals, also noted that "lying on the back and exposing the throat is the attitude and the signal of submission among wolves and other canines." Dr. Smith put this to a test with a wild male wolf. When the animal growled threateningly, Smith lay down and exposed his throat. "The wolf touched my throat with his teeth in the typical canine caress. I wasn't bitten, but I was almost scared to death," he said.

In analyzing video-tape-recorded confrontations, we have observed a higher frequency of agreement among men with their coats unbuttoned than with those whose coats remained buttoned. Many men who have their arms folded on their chest in a defensive gesture also will have their jackets buttoned. Someone who has just favorably changed his mind might uncross his arms and instinctively unbutton his coat. Keep him in that position and your mutual objectives will probably be more easily reached.

Countless times when negotiations were going well we

have recorded a "getting together" gesture-cluster: Seated individuals unbutton their coats, uncross their legs, and move up toward the edge of the chair and closer to the desk or table that separates them from their opposer. This gesture-cluster is in most instances accompanied by verbal language that communicates a possible agreement, solution, or generally a positive expression of working together for the needs of both.

At a party given by her husband's family, a newlywed noted how difficult it was for her to distinguish the family from the nonfamily members. She was told to try looking at the nonverbal communications. Then she was asked to identify each individual present as a friend or as a member of the family. In ten tries she made the right selection eight times by simply noting which ones had their coats off or unbuttoned. The two persons about whom she guessed incorrectly were a longtime friend who had been attending family functions for over twenty years (coat unbuttoned) and a family member who very seldom attended such functions and generally was a "loner" (coat buttoned).

## Defensiveness

> "An attitude not only of defence,
> but defiance."
> —Thomas Gillespie, "The Mountain Storm"

In contrast to gestures that indicate openness are those that guard the body or the emotions against a threatened assault. If openness is mishandled, it can easily become defensiveness.

Arms Crossed on Chest. Any baseball fan knows exactly what to expect when an umpire makes a call that is not accepted by a team manager. The manager runs out on the field toward the umpire, arms swinging or hands deeply thrust in his back pockets, probably formed into fists, and the umpire,

**14.   The crossed-arms defensive position**

seeing the manager, crosses his arms in a gesture of defensiveness (Figure 14). (An exception is the plate umpire: He does
not cross his arms on his chest—he already has a chest pro-
tector.) By the time the manager reaches him, the umpire
has clearly communicated that he is prepared to defend his
decision, and the manager argues to no avail. As part of his
defensive gesture-cluster, the umpire may turn his back to the
manager, signaling, "You've argued too much."

The crossed-arm position is a common occurrence in everyday life and, according to Darwin, seems to be used throughout the world to communicate defensiveness. Teachers use it,
especially when in a group of their peers, and doctors tend to
use it when in the company of other doctors. The very young
will cross their arms when defying their parents' instructions,
and the very old when they are defending their right to be

heard. It seemingly acts as a protective guard against an anticipated attack or a fixed position from which the individual would rather not move.

Of all the indicators we have researched, this gesture tends to be the easiest to understand and sometimes the least recognized as a nonverbal indicator. It also tends to be a gesture that influences the behavior of others. In a group of four or more persons, you can influence the entire group by crossing your arms in a defensive position. Hold this gesture not only when listening but when speaking and notice how soon other members of the group follow your lead. Once two of you have assumed and are holding this fixed position, the other members are also affected. You will find it very easy to divide the group into subgroups or cause individuals to assume positions that are difficult to reverse to achieve open communication.

The crossed-arms gesture is quite common in our video-tape recordings of negotiations. Unfortunately, many individuals are unaware that when their opposer crosses his arms, he is signaling that he has become defensive. Only when viewing the video tape does the participant realize his mistake. Instead of drawing out the opposer's feelings by relating to him and finding out what his needs are, the trainee has continued the same discourse that caused the opposer to become defensive in the first place. People often very effectively "turn off" and continue to turn off the person they would like to "turn on." When we observe our opposer with his arms crossed, we should reconsider whatever we are doing or saying to that individual. He is strongly communicating that he has withdrawn from the conversation.

Very frequently a postmortem on video-recorded negotiations that have failed reveals that a demand, request, or offer was made at a time or in such a manner as to cause the other person to become defensive. From this point on, concessions, agreements, or other forms of cooperation become more difficult. Failing to recognize early signs of disagreement,

**15.    Fists reinforcing the defensive position**

discomfort, or discontent will usually lead to a more com-
plicated situation in which agreement on any issue will prove
to be almost painful.

If you should be in a situation in which you wonder whether
the individual is defensive or assuming a position of comfort
(as some argue), notice the hands. Are they relaxed or fistlike
(Figure 15)? Are the fingers wrapped around the bicep in a

stranglehold to the extent that the knuckles become white (Figure 16)? Such protective posture is like that of the infrequent and nervous air traveler who grips the armrests of his seat during takeoff, his hands tense.

**16. The arm-gripping defensive position**

Since women have an upper-torso structure that differs from men's, they fold their arms considerably lower on the body (Figure 17). Girls entering puberty assume this protective position with a far greater frequency than their older sisters.

**17.   A woman's way with the crossed-arms gesture**

**18. Indifference or worse: a leg over arm of chair**

Sitting with a Leg over Arm of Chair ("getting a leg up") (Figure 18). At first we assumed that it was a comfortable position from which a person communicated by his openness a certain amount of cooperative spirit. However, we soon dis-

19.   Straddling a chair, another domineering pose

46

covered that despite the seemingly relaxed position, the person —even if he sometimes has a slight smile on his face—is not cooperative. Instead he is generally unconcerned about or hostile to the other person's feelings or needs. We also uncovered a similar body position in Henry Siddons's book, *Rhetorical Gestures,* in which Siddons describes as "indifferent" an English country gentleman of 1832 sitting in this very position. Airline stewardesses have reported that male travelers who take this position are often difficult to relate to. In many buyer/seller relationships, the buyer in his office will take this position to announce nonverbally his dominance or territorial rights in the encounter on his homeground, and many a boss will assume it to show superiority in his employee's office.

Sitting with the Chair Back Serving as a Shield (Figure 19). This position and feet on top of desk closely parallel what we have just described. To a great extent they occur during superior/subordinate situations. We again caution that despite the seemingly informal and cooperative positions your opposer takes, all may not be as it seems. He is attempting to show dominance or aggression.

Crossing Legs. If you were to stroll by the many sidewalk cafés in any European country, you could probably pick out a male American tourist simply from the way his legs are crossed. The European male crosses leg over leg. The American male uses what Birdwhistell describes as "figure-four," one leg horizontally crossed with the ankle resting on the other knee (Figure 20). Apparently this is strictly an American way of sitting, and even many American women, when wearing slacks, adopt it.

A recent seminar attendee remarked that his wife, who was

20. The European manner of crossing legs and the distinctly American figure-four position

born and educated in Europe, constantly belittled him for sitting in the "figure-four" position. She often asked, "Why don't you sit like a gentleman?" To this he retorted, "I am!" It wasn't until he attended the seminar that the significance of her complaint was made clear. She meant, "Why don't you sit like a European gentleman?" (We conducted a seminar for a British firm in Manchester, England. Out of eighty-three executives only two sat in the "figure-four" position at any time during the program.)

Another seminar attendee, one who had served with German Intelligence during World War II, commented on the number of American agents who were caught as a result of eating with the fork in the right hand in spite of careful training in eating in the European style. We noted that twice as many could have been caught if German Intelligence had looked for the figure-four position. In our more than two thousand recorded confrontations where one or both opposers crossed their legs in this manner, in almost every instance it signaled that the confrontation had reached a highly competitive stage. A friend of ours in London, a fine chess player who was educated in the United States, has often remarked that he invariably takes a figure-four position when the match is in doubt. He agrees that it is a foolish position for a chess player to take, for every time it is his turn he must uncross his legs and move forward. However, he adds that when the match is no longer in doubt and he feels secure in winning, he places both feet on the floor.

We have observed in our recordings that quite frequently during the stage of the negotiation when issues are being presented and discussed or when a heated argument is taking place, one or both of the negotiators have their legs crossed— either in leg-over-leg or in the American figure-four style. We observed that the number of negotiations where settlements were reached increased greatly when both negotiators had uncrossed their legs and moved toward each other. In our recordings of such confrontations, we cannot recall one situation that resulted in a settlement where even one of the negotiators still had his legs crossed. Individuals who cross their legs seem to be the ones who give you the most competition and need the greatest amount of attention. In further verification, we discussed the crossed-leg, leaning-away position with numerous salesmen. None could recall being able to close a sale with the prospect in that position. If crossed legs are coupled with crossed arms, you really have an adversary.

When a woman crosses her legs and moves her foot in a slight kicking motion, she is probably bored with the situation —waiting for a plane to depart, a husband who is late, or listening to dull talk (Figure 21).

**21.   Boredom or impatience**

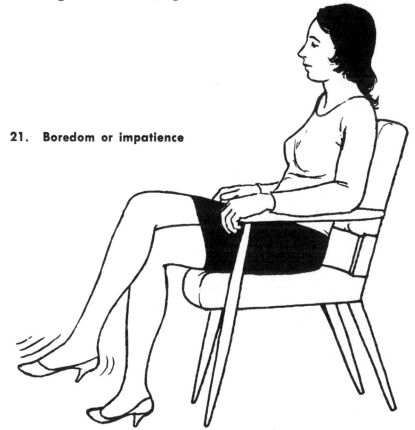

## Evaluation

"When a student in a classroom becomes
really absorbed in the problem at hand, he
is likely to slip down on his shoulder blades,
spread his feet, ruffle his hair and do any
number of unconventional deeds. Let the
spell be broken, and he sits up, rearranges his
clothes and again becomes socially proper."
—C. H. Woolbert, "The Audience"

Some of the most misinterpreted gestures are what we call
evaluation gestures—those dealing with pensiveness or thought-
fulness. Since much of our effectiveness in business and social
life depends on communications, knowledge and appraisal of
feedback information are vital for the individual who wants to
know how well his message has been received. Very little
research has been conducted on the evaluation process before
the acceptance of an idea, product, or service. However, we
have accumulated a considerable amount of data on gestures
from the behavioral patterns of salesmen, teachers, nurses,
executives, lawyers, and many others, indicating that there
are actions that *do* communicate that persons are evaluating.
For clarification, let us look at a classroom situation.

Mrs. Clark, who teaches math, is explaining an essential
aspect of the subject. She notices that Fred is staring at her
with unblinking eyes, his body taut and erect, his feet flat on
the floor. She discerns no motion whatever from Fred. Do you
think that Fred is listening to the lecture, evaluating what Mrs.
Clark is saying? If you think he *is* interested, you are wrong.
A young teacher unaccustomed to this posture might fall for
it, but a more experienced educator would not. Fred has turned
his teacher off and is using a cover-up technique to convince
her that he is "all ears."

Ignoring Fred's trance, Mrs. Clark turns to Charles. He is

**22. Evaluation gestures**

sitting toward the edge of his chair, his body leaning forward, and his head, slightly tilted, is supported by one hand. Mrs. Clark would be correct in judging that Charles is interested.

Hand-to-Cheek Gestures (Figure 22). Auguste Rodin, the great sculptor, showed deep insight into gestural language when he created "The Thinker." Who would doubt that his sculpture is of a person thoroughly engrossed in working out a problem? Persons who strike poses similar to Rodin's "Thinker," with hand on cheek, are involved in some sort of meditation. Sometimes there is a slight blinking of the eyes. A youngster sitting on a staircase looking down at adults assumes this position, as do many, young and old, when sitting on a curb watching a parade.

This position of interest and attentiveness has been recognized by a friend who makes audio-visual presentations to his management team. When he stands in the back of the room he can estimate how well he is conducting a presentation by the number of executives who have one or both hands to their head and are leaning forward, as opposed to those sitting back in their chair with their legs crossed, arms folded, or bodies twisted away from the screen.

Sometimes a person assumes what we refer to as a "critical-evaluation cluster" (Figure 23). He brings a hand to his face, puts his chin in the palm, and extends his index finger along his cheek; the remaining fingers are positioned below the mouth. When these hand-to-cheek gestures are associated with the body drawn back from the other individual, the thought patterns are critical, cynical, or in some other way negative toward the person attempting to persuade.

When conducting our seminars, one of the first gestures we look for to determine how difficult the group might be are these types of hand-to-cheek poses. If we have, say, fifty executives in attendance, during the first fifteen minutes—

**23.  A critical evaluation**

especially during a nonverbal-communication presentation—
at least thirty will be sitting in some kind of hand-to-face
position. Of this number, approximately one-half will be very
interested in what is being said and will lean forward slightly.
The other half will take more of a wait-and-see attitude and
will sit back, a bit skeptical of what is being said. The remaining twenty will be divided roughly among those sitting
with their arms crossed (show me) and those sitting on the
edge of the chair, elbows on thighs and hands hanging loose
("This is great! Let me play, coach"). Our job is to change
evaluation into interest.

Head Tilted.    Charles Darwin noticed early in his studies
that animals as well as men tend to cock their heads slightly
whenever they hear something that interests them. From a
very early age, women instinctively understand the significance
of this gesture: It gives the impression of listening intently.
They use it consciously when conversing with a male whom
they want to impress—and they do.

In our seminars, if most of the participants' heads are not
tilted we feel that the group as a whole has not become
interested in our material. Once the speaker is aware of this
gesture, he can relate to his audience in a more positive
manner and can gauge how well his information is getting
across. This can be especially helpful when the speaker wants
to cover a great deal of material in a very short time. When
an electrical circuit is overloaded a breaker opens so that the
circuit does not take more energy than it can handle. Individuals sometimes behave in the same manner toward
information-overloading. They gesture their indifference to
additional data. The clusters change. Heads become erect
rather than tilted, backs straighten up, then slouch. There
are glances at the ceiling, at watches, at others, and finally
some will start positioning their bodies so that they are pointing toward the exit. If the group has reached this stage, the
speaker should understand that they are nonverbally signaling
"Enough."

**24. The chin-stroking evaluation gesture**

Stroking Chin (thinking/evaluating) (Figure 24). This "Well, let me consider" gesture, which seems to be world-wide, is made when people go through a decision-making process. Probably every Western movie has had a scene in which a bewhiskered frontier doctor stroked his chin and said, "I don't know, Marshal, if that's the best way to handle them Daltons." In the musical *Fiddler on the Roof*, whenever Tevye is thinking over something important, he invariably strokes his beard. Darwin refers to meditation gestures and reports that various people throughout the world "sometimes pull on their beards . . . hands, usually the thumb and index finger, in contact with some part of the face, commonly the upper lip." Henry Siddons's *Rhetorical Gestures* states, "This gesture signifies the wise man making a judgment."

On stage, particularly in Shakespearean theater, an actor can be seen performing this action congruent with words that

**25. "What was that again?"**

communicate careful study or analysis. Watching a chess match, one can frequently observe this gesture in the player required to make the next move. After a decision is made, the stroking stops—and not merely because he has to use his hand. Many businessmen use this gesture, though some attempt to conceal it by making only a very slight stroking motion.

A congruent facial expression with this gesture is a slight squinting of the eyes, as if trying to see an answer to the problem in the distance.

Gestures with Glasses. An evaluating gesture that causes a negative emotional reaction in others is the one of dropping eyeglasses onto the lower bridge of the nose and peering over them (Figure 25). The recipient of the stare feels that he is being closely scrutinized and looked down upon. Many executives who wear "granny" glasses for reading purposes are especially likely to elicit this reaction inadvertently from subordinates. We urge that if this happens to be one of your traits, be aware of the negative aspects. Better yet, try not to do it for a while and see if you do not get a favorable reaction.

Next is what we call the procrastination, or pausing-for-thought gesture. A very common variety is very slowly and deliberately taking the glasses off and carefully cleaning the lenses, even though the glasses may not need it. Some perform this ritual as many as four or five times an hour. We have video-recorded the gesture many times in negotiation confrontations. In most instances the person wanted to delay or stall for time to think over his situation before either raising more opposition, asking for clarification, or posing a question.

A similar gesture to gain time is one in which the glasses are removed and the earpiece of the frame is put in the mouth (Figure 26). Since people cannot speak very well with objects in their mouth, they might do a better job of listening or avoid saying anything when they want to think about it first. Putting things in the mouth also implies that the person is seeking nourishment, possibly in the form of more information.

**26.  Gaining time to evaluate**

Another member of the family of gestures in which glasses are used is taking them off, either quickly or with much emphasis, and throwing them on the table. A negotiator whom we know always signals his emotional outbreaks in this way. How many people use this gesture consciously as an expression of "Now you're going too far" or "Just wait a damn minute" will probably never be known. However, most people, regardless of whether they are aware of their gesture, are communicating resistance to what is being said. Therefore, if you encounter this gesture in another person, change your approach. Do something to relieve the emotional tension. Get that person back to wearing his glasses so that both of you can "see" different alternatives.

Pipe-Smokers.   Pipe-smokers are necessarily more involved with the ritual of smoking than are cigarette-smokers. After all, the pipe-smoker has many more functions to perform: He has to fill the pipe, clean it, tap it, stoke it, and keep it lit. In the process he can use it as a scratcher, pointer, drumstick, etc., which permits the use of the pipe (to stall for thinking time) as a secret signal instrument. We have an associate whom we call "the Toscanini of the pipe-smokers." He conducts negotiation signals with his pipe like the maestro conducted the NBC Symphony. Our associate, an inveterate pipe-smoker, has devised an intricate series of pipe signals. They communicate such instructions to his team as *shut up, listen more closely, the offer stinks,* and *let's go.* It is of great assistance in a team negotiation to have signals by which you can communicate nonverbally, with or without a pipe.

One can often observe the deliberate motions the pipe-smoker goes through when he is fighting or maneuvering for time to think or reconsider. We have observed that a considerable number of pipe-smokers are engineers or scientists or are in other technical fields where abstract thinking is vitally important. They take considerably more time in decision-making than the more factually oriented thinkers, who tend to smoke cigarettes.

In our video-tape recordings of business confrontations, a distinct personality type emerges both for the cigarette- and the pipe-smoker. The pipe-smoker tends to play "cat and mouse" or "hide and seek" as long as he possibly can without revealing his position. On the other hand, the cigarette-smoker's attitude is generally "Let's get this over with and go on to other things." Pipe-smokers give the impression that they are more patient and conservative than cigarette-smokers, who generally look like sprinters ready for action. (The ratio of cigarette-smokers to pipe-smokers who have participated in our research is 10–1, which is not unusual considering that an overwhelming number of businessmen tend to be of the concrete rather than abstract variety of thinker.)

Pacing. Americans seem to feel more comfortable thinking on their foot. They frequently resort to this mannerism when attempting to solve a hard problem or make a difficult decision. As gestures go, this is a very positive one. But one should not speak to the pacer. It might cause him to lose his trend of thought and interfere with what he is trying to decide. Most sales-oriented people understand how important it is to let a prospective client or customer alone while he is pacing and deciding whether to buy. They let him interrupt the silence if he wants to pose an objection or question. Many successful negotiations have resulted from one person biting his tongue and not uttering a word while the other goes through his decision-making, rug-pacing ritual.

Pinching the Bridge of the Nose (Figure 27). This gesture, usually accompanied with closed eyes, communicates great thought and concern about the decision to be made. A person in self-conflict might lower his head and pinch the bridge of his nose to test whether he really is in such a predicament or it is only a bad dream. A businessman we know clearly signals

**27.   "It's hard for me to see the answer."**

his quandary by this gesture. When he performs it, we merely keep quiet and wait for him to raise his objections to what is being discussed. We do not attempt to reason him out of this situation. Instead we recognize his feelings and wait for him to express his doubts.

An attorney who attended one of our seminars commented that a judge he knew usually signaled his feelings about a case by this gesture. If the judge believed the defendant was guilty, he seldom removed his glasses. However, if he believed the accused was innocent, he performed this gesture openly and sometimes kept his eyes closed several minutes, fighting with his assumptions and feelings about the guilt of the accused.

From these evaluation-clusters it is easy to progress to the next attitude—suspicion and secretiveness.

## Suspicion and Secretiveness

> **"There are many wise men, that have secret
> hearts, and transparent countenances."**
> **—Francis Bacon**

Gestures that connote suspicion or secretiveness are sometimes referred to as "left-handed" gestures. This reflects the American slang meaning of "undesirable," as in a "left-handed" ship, compliment, or honeymoon. Interestingly, in sign language the right thumb extended upward means *good*, but the left little finger means *evil*. This additional mode of communication recognizes a right (good) and left (bad) connotation.

At a recent meeting, one of our colleagues was being extremely reticent about stating his position, which was different from ours. Every time we approached what seemed to be the sensitive area, his left hand came up to cover his mouth either prior to or while he spoke. Not wanting to make him any more uncomfortable than he already was, we asked questions that might cause him to let go and tell us what his feelings were. At last, when asked a "Do you really feel that way about it?" type of question, he replied by stating that his "heart was not in it" and used other such phrases. His gestures were based on his strong opposition to our objectives. He had attempted to hide his true feelings and go along with our ideas. Had we *not* been aware of what he was truly communicating, a solution would have been reached that in the long run might have proven to be very unfavorable for all of us. There are many people who say things they believe you want them to say. Afterward they feel extremely frustrated with themselves because they have not exposed their true feelings and, as a result, often work against the goals rather than trying to achieve them.

If a person tends *not* to look at you at all, he is very likely to be concealing something. However, incongruity in gesture-clusters probably is the best indication of a person being secretive. A smiling, belligerent, defensive person is incongruous and may be, with a superficial smile, attempting to soften the blow. "One may smile, and smile, and be a villain," as Shakespeare says in *Hamlet*. Similarly, even those without nonverbal training or conscious exposure to it sense when someone is playing a game of hide and seek. What most have difficulty in doing is to isolate the gestures that have communicated this awareness and then to understand how to cope with the situation creatively.

All the gestures that communicate suspicion, uncertainty, rejection, and doubt essentially have a common message: negative! The emphasis differs, as do the accompanying emotions, but the signal is usually loud and clear: "I'm not buying."

A certain portion of what we say to others is received with suspicion, uncertainty, rejection, and doubt. When they feel this way about what we are saying, they nonverbally feed back their attitude. The most obvious gestures of the rejection-cluster are folded arms, moving the body away, crossed legs, and tilting the head forward, with the person either peering over his glasses or squinting as if trying to *see* what is said more clearly. The more subtle gestures that sometimes escape our awareness include turning the body only slightly away so as to present a silhouette and the nose-touching or -rubbing gesture. These probably account for most of the negative feelings.

Sideways Glance (Figure 28). Do you register it as suspicion and doubt when people give you the sideways glance? There is a common phrase, "She gave me a cold shoulder." It confirms the gesture we associate with a distrusting attitude. Can you specifically recall instances when someone said something to you that you did not like, did not agree with, or in general were very doubtful of? Did you take a sideways position while saying something like, "What do you mean by that?" It is similar to a boxer or fencer getting ready to square off with

**28. "Just what do you mean?"**

his opponent. Try to help an old lady who would rather cross the street by herself and you will discover exactly what the expression means—a forty-five-degree turn of the body away from you. It is a gesture of rejection even without a "No, thank you."

Feet and/or Entire Body Pointing toward the Exit (see Figure 24). In many situations you will notice that suddenly someone has shifted his body and is sitting so that his feet are pointing toward a door. This gesture is a clear sign that the person wishes to end the meeting, conversation, or whatever is going on. His body-shifting is telling you he is anxious to leave. But it is one thing to be aware of this gesture and another to do something about it. Either do something different to get the individual to turn toward you and lean forward or let him go. It does you no good in the long run to keep talking to someone who is telling you that he is anxious to leave.

It is indeed an observant subordinate who is able to read his boss's gesture when it means that the meeting is at an end. If the employee is aware of this signal and lets his boss leave, he will have assisted his employer, which will be appreciated. However, if he delays his superior, the boss will resent it and thereafter close his mind to everything the employee says.

People visiting you socially make similar signals. Sometime during the last half-hour of their visit they start positioning their bodies as if to leave. A smart host or hostess notices this signal and may sincerely say, "It's getting late. Time certainly passes quickly when we are together." Even if you get verbal disagreement, you may notice that after you have spoken they move their bodies toward the edge of the chair as a further endorsement that they really *do* want to leave.

Touching or Slightly Rubbing the Nose, Usually with Index Finger (Figure 29).   Once a young man was discussing books with Professor Birdwhistell at the University of Louisville. When asked his opinion of one modern classic, the young man rubbed his nose and said he had enjoyed the book very much. "The truth is," said the professor, "you didn't like the book." Trapped by the comment and yet not sure of how he had given himself away, he admitted that he had in fact read only a few pages and "found them all dull." He had rubbed his nose in front of the wrong man.

Birdwhistell and others have decided that the nose-rub among Americans is as much a sign of rejection as "No!" Our finding is that nose-touching or -rubbing is a doubt sign and in many cases that doubt is expressing the same thing Birdwhistell discovered: "No!" Ask an adolescent a question that he has difficulty in answering and watch how quickly his index finger goes through the touching/rubbing action. Most of us

**29. Touching the nose**

have no difficulty in recognizing this youngster's gesture as an expression of doubt. However, when the same signal is given by a forty-year-old associate or neighbor, we often do not see it at all.

On a television interview show, a well-known news commentator was asked, "What will historians think of today's youth and their ideals?" The commentator, who most likely had been trained to keep his hands away from his face when speaking, still brought his index finger to the side of his nose, then said, "I believe historians will see today's youth as the greatest patriots this country has ever had." If the nose-touching/rubbing gesture communicates doubt or negation, then how might the commentator's doubts be viewed? (1) Whether to answer the question at all. (2) Whether he really believed what he was about to say. (3) Doubt as to how to best communicate his belief. (4) Doubt on how the viewing audience would receive what he was about to say. In reading the other gestures he had given, plus the congruity of his overall posture, we believe that his doubt was (4), over how his audience would react to what he was about to say. Why? His previous gesture-clusters were steepling, sitting in an open position, leaning forward, and other clusters showing great openness and confidence. This eliminated (1) and (2). Only this particular question caused him to touch his nose and move back in his seat. He had shown no previous doubt as to the best way to answer any other question. This eliminated (3).

This gesture is not uncommon. It is used by many articulate speakers at times when they are not sure how to approach a subject or what the audience reaction to it might be. A seminar attendee stated that in negotiations in which he had participated he put all his offers and counteroffers "on the nose of his opposer." He explained that the main gesture he observed was his opposer's touching his nose. This action signaled how far or near they were to a settlement. He found that at the outset, when both were jockeying for position, his opposer touched his nose often while speaking or listening. As the negotiation proceeded he saw less nose-touching, and finally, when he made a counteroffer, his opposer, instead of touching his nose, moved up toward the edge of the chair. A settlement followed. In a postmortem of what had happened, he made notes of the significance of this gesture in relation to offers or counteroffers. He found that in almost every instance when his opposer had touched his nose the gesture preceded or followed an offer or counteroffer.

A word of warning for those who might take any gesture as absolute: Sometimes people rub their nose because it itches.

However, there is a distinct difference between the mannerism of rubbing one's nose due to an itch and rubbing it as a gesture of negation or doubt. Persons rubbing (or scratching) their nose usually do it vigorously, whereas those making the other gesture do it very lightly. The latter is subtle and often accompanied by a gesture-cluster, such as squirming in the chair, twisting the body into a silhouette position, or physically withdrawing. Other variations of this gesture are rubbing behind or beside the ear with the index finger (Figure 30) when

30.   "Well, I don't know."

weighing an answer, very commonly coupled with "Well, I don't know," and rubbing the eye (Figure 31)—another frequent sign of doubt.

**31.    "I can't see it."**

# CHAPTER 4

# Readiness, Reassurance, Cooperation, Frustration

> "The foulest, the vilest, the obscenest
> picture the world possesses—Titian's
> Venus. It isn't that she is naked and
> stretched out on a bed—no, it is the attitude
> of one of her arms and hand."
> —Mark Twain, "A Tramp Abroad"

In this chapter, as in the previous one, the positive, constructive attitudes are contrasted with the negative ones. At the same time, every other attitude has emotional similarities with those preceding it and following it. A comparison of their similarities and differences will enable you to more readily appreciate the attitude described.

## Readiness

> "One quickly gets readiness in an art where
> strong desire comes in play."
> —Thomas Mann

Some people equate readiness with aggressiveness. We will, however, use "readiness" in relation to a goal-oriented high achiever who usually has no time for hostility, since he is busy gathering information and getting things done. He is a person who has a high enthusiasm for what he is attempting to achieve and may also have some of the qualities that Dr. Abraham Maslow has described as "self-actualizing." It is in this broad context that we approach the readiness gesture-clusters we have researched and recorded.

Hands on Hips (Figure 32). This is the first of the overt gestures we can clearly identify. You often see it during a sports event when an athlete is waiting to become involved. At a business meeting someone standing with his hands on his hips with feet spread apart is in all probability interested in having the attendees follow his direction. Notice how a young son or daughter stands the next time one of them challenges his parents' authority. Notice also your own standing position when you are enthusiastically pursuing a goal that you believe to be worthwhile.

Many of us, regardless of age or sex, take the hands-on-hips position. A high achiever often does so as he nonverbally communicates his dedication to a goal. With some, the gesture that accompanies the hands-on-hips stance is hitching up the trousers, as a well-known professional golfer is often seen doing. You will also note that when the hands are placed on the hips the legs are apart, as it is difficult to maintain balance if the feet are together. A variation of this gesture is a seated person with one hand on his mid-thigh and leaning slightly forward (Figure 33).

Think for a moment about someone you know well who normally assumes the hands-on-hips position. Is that person by your definition goal-oriented? Does he enjoy competition? For several years we have kept a record of executives who have attended our seminars. Approximately 75 percent of them will, when asking a question during the first hour of the seminar, assume a hands-on-hips position with their coats off or unbuttoned.

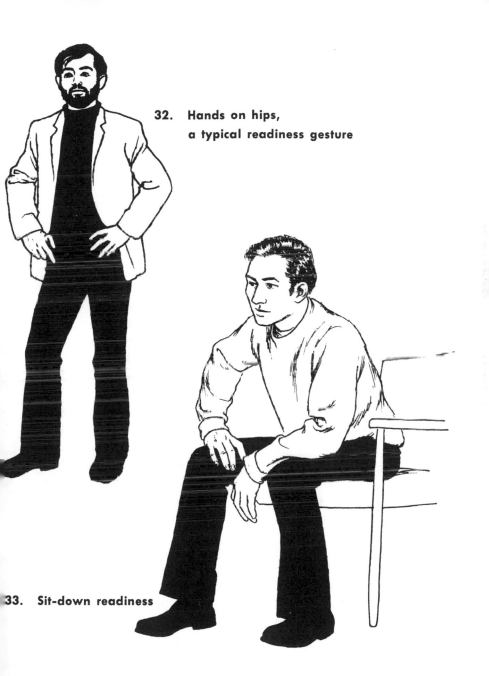

**32. Hands on hips,
a typical readiness gesture**

**33. Sit-down readiness**

71

This gesture is one in which an individual communicates his desire to be ready and able. Since it is a positive gesture, there is no cause for concern on your part, and if you, too, are a goal-oriented person, you can share his feelings. This may help you to reach a mutually desired goal.

Sitting on Edge of Chair ("He had them on the edge of their seats"). In many video-tape recordings we have observed that persons have moved toward the edge of the chair when getting ready to compromise, cooperate, buy, accept, or concur—or conclude, reject, or leave. This indicates that an overt movement is completely oriented toward *action*. Remember the last time you signed a contract? You were probably sitting on the edge of your chair several minutes before you agreed to the terms and conditions. If you did not like the deal, you probably used the same gesture to signal your feelings to the salesman before you finally had the courage to get up and leave. Many knowledgeable persons in sales with whom we have discussed this position agree that people do communicate their eagerness to buy by sitting on the edge of their seats. They also concur that after a person has offered them a great deal of sales resistar e and then shifts to the edge of his chair, he is ready to get up and leave. This is the time for the coup de grace if a lost sale is to be recaptured. If the salesman does not have something new to regain the customer's interest, he might better spend his time tackling another potential client.

Arms Spread While Hands Grip Edge of Table (Figure 34). This is a strong "Listen to me, damn it, I have something to say" position while sitting or standing. Picture the situation where the subordinate takes this position and says to his superior, "You can't fire me, I quit." This condition can lead to a terrible predicament if you do not recognize the gesture and the emotions that are about to be released by the other person. Displayed by your child, employee, boss, customer—

**34. The showdown**

or whomever—it should be recognized and accommodated. One should not stretch out another's emotions to the point where they will snap. We have noted in video-tape recordings that when one of the negotiators takes this overt position, the other is often completely oblivious to his nonverbal message. The result invariably is an emotional upheaval that can be very destructive.

Moving In, Speaking Confidentially. A more subtle gesture-cluster indicates an aggressive readiness covertly. It is used as a cover to dominate or direct another person. The gesturer usually leans toward you, moving into an intimacy distance of about thirteen inches (Americans normally converse at from twenty-three to twenty-five inches). While imparting this sensation of physical closeness, such a person often lowers his voice and gives the impression that what he is saying is confidential and only for your ears. On the contrary, the gesture signals that he is used to having his direction followed and will physically attempt to dominate others in this manner.

You have probably seen the situation in a cartoon where a taller character attempts to dominate the shorter one by narrowing the distance between them. You can imagine the tall one saying, "And what I want you to do is . . ." However, there are some who accept this "narrowing the distance between us" gesture as an endorsement and are in no manner offended by it. If you should use the gesture, be alert to these diametrically opposed reactions. It may not communicate what you mean at all.

## Reassurance

Seeing yourself on television for the first time can be traumatic, as it adds about ten pounds, makes a generous amount of hair look like a toupee, and ages those who wear glasses. And since most people are their own worst critics, they tend to be dissatisfied with their appearance and performance.

It has been the policy at our seminars to have a trial run before video-taping an actual negotiating confrontation. We record those who have never been on video tape and let them see it before they are taped at the negotiating session. This is done primarily to melt away any apprehension they may have about facing a television camera. As Walter Pater says, "The way to perfection is through a series of disgusts." During these first viewings we have collected a great deal of data on reassurance gesture-clusters because each viewer wanted to convince himself that "it wasn't *too* bad."

Seeking reassurance from a blanket or other object is not confined to Linus in the "Peanuts" comic strip or children of that age. In adults, clenched hands with the thumbs rubbing against each other is one of the most common gestures we have observed. Variations are cuticle-picking and hand-pinching. Another gesture is sticking a pen or pencil in the mouth to chew or suck. Sometimes a scrap of paper or a paperclip serves the purpose. Another reassurance gesture, observed by Dr. James Enneis, of St. Elizabeth's Hospital, is touching the back of a chair before sitting down at a conference. Enneis describes it as "reassuring themselves that they belong."

A very common gesture of reassurance when a woman says or hears something that makes her uncomfortable is to slowly and gracefully bring her hand to her throat. When she is wearing a necklace the movement is disguised as wanting to feel that the necklace is still there. If you ask her, "Are you sure about what you just said?" she will probably attempt to assure you that she is, or she will become defensive and refuse to answer. In either case, she is signaling that she does not completely believe what she has said.

Another common gesture that communicates reassurance is pinching the fleshy part of the hand. It is used by both men and women, though it is far more common with women. In one test we furnished first viewers with coffee to try to keep their hands occupied while they watched the playback. We wanted to see how many would set the coffee down and then go through a self-pinching gesture. We found that many of them first used the cup as a shield in front of their eyes, as though trying to block out the offending sight, then set it down and went through the self-pinching ritual.

Various finger gestures convey one's anxieties, inner conflicts, or apprehension. A child needing reassurance sucks his thumb, a teen-ager concerned about exams bites his nails, and a taxpayer worried about April 15 picks at his cuticles until they are sore. Sometimes adolescents and adults substitute other objects for fingers and use pens and pencils for their biting gestures. Others do not like the plastic, metal, or wooden taste, so they switch to paper or even fabrics.

If we can supply assurance where needed, our opposer can be made cooperative.

## Cooperation

"We are born for cooperation, as are the
feet, the hands, the eyelids, and the upper
and lower jaws."
                                        —Marcus Aurelius

Who are the persons who genuinely want to cooperate and
how do they communicate their willingness? Recently we were
a part of a negotiating team discussing a product of great
scientific value. The issues involved were patent rights, equity
position, royalties, research and development costs, and in-
centives for both our client and the company that was to
manufacture and market the product. As soon as the discussion
started, one of the opposer's team members took a sprinter's
position (sitting forward in chair, feet on tiptoes), nonverbally
communicating he was ready for action. As he was the scientific member of the opposer's team, a great deal depended on
his reaction to our overall presentation. Initially, his "ready
for action" posture told us that he probably favored our
product. His technical questions and doubts were brought out
in the open and expertly answered by our client's scientific
staff member. We purposely sat next to this man in the hope
that after we had answered his questions and satisfied his
doubts he would favorably influence the other members of
his team. We read him well. He became extremely cooperative
and served as our ally. Recognizing this individual's cooperative gestures and capitalizing on them brought about a successful conclusion that benefited both parties.

Undoubtedly there have been times when you sensed that
someone was cooperating fully until suddenly something went
wrong. He had been calling you by your first name but now
he addressed you formally. His smile had become a frown. The
corners of his lips turned down. There were wrinkles in his

brow, and perhaps he glared at you with downward-tilted eyebrows. You probably felt completely inadequate to cope with such an abrupt change in attitude.

In such situations many of us attempt to determine what went wrong but usually in very general terms: "He didn't like my idea," or "Boy, did he get uptight about my request." Instead of this Monday-morning quarterbacking we should attempt to restructure the conversation and the attendant gestures at the moment the person ceased to be cooperative. Oftentimes we find it very difficult to believe that *we* might have been unreasonable and so precipitated the crisis. The observant person sees this chip-on-shoulder, folded-arms stage approaching by observing the statements, speech inflection, and facial expressions and other gestures that precede it. It is then possible to head off a serious confrontation and restore the cooperative environment that had existed before the break. Better yet, do not let the change from cooperation to resistance even occur. Instead, monitor how the person is reacting by observing his gestures and, at the first negative indication, immediately re-evaluate what you have been communicating. The following are some cooperative gesture-clusters to be aware of:

Sitting on Edge of Chair. This is a cooperative gesture if it is congruous with gesture-clusters communicating interest in what you are saying. An example is the case of a buyer showing his eagerness to sign a contract and shifting his weight toward the edge of the chair.

Hand-to-Face Gestures. These can communicate anything from boredom to evaluative interest. Evaluation can become favorable, therefore it can be considered a gesture that communicates a degree of cooperation. Given a choice of ten people sitting with their legs crossed versus ten with their hands to their heads, we would chose the hand-to-head group as potentially more cooperative.

Unbuttoning of Coat.   This gesture seems not only to communicate that a person is opening up to you and your ideas but that he is concentrating on what you are saying.

Tilted Head.   This gesture is cooperative to the extent that the person is interested in what you are saying. He has not turned you off.

## Frustration

> "A frown, a spoken word, or a kick is a
> message that a sender conveys by means
> of his own current bodily activity, the
> transmission occurring only during the time
> that his body is present to sustain
> this activity."
> —Erving Goffman, "Behavior in Public Places"

If you happen to be watching a football game on television, chances are that you will see a familiar scene. The quarterback fades back and throws a pass that goes in and out of his teammate's hands. The teammate's emotional reaction to missing the pass is to kick the ground, slap the side of his helmet, then do a double karate chop at the air. His baseball-playing counterpart (Figure 35) might gesture his frustration by removing his hat, running his fingers through his hair, rubbing the back of his neck, then kicking the dirt (or nothing in particular).

The businessman who is desperately trying to convince his customer that the shipment is en route ("Get off my back") might go through the same hair- and back-of-the-neck-rubbing. If on the phone, he may pick up a pencil and either throw it with force or break it in two.

Short Breaths.   Some gestures combine movement with sound effects. The bull snorts when he is angry. People who

**35. The frustrated baseball player**

are furious usually take short breaths and expel the air through
their nostrils in spurts similar to snorting. In a sorrowful situation, highly emotional people take deep breaths and expel the
air slowly, making long, sighing sounds. Breathing also plays
a prominent part in the communication of frustration and
disgust. For example, Helen has just been summoned by her
boss to discuss why she persists in making mistakes in adding
up customers' charges. Helen's boss starts out by taking a deep
breath, then says, "How many times have we warned you
about these errors?" As Helen explains that she is not very
good at arithmetic and that an adding machine should be
made available, her boss takes the suggestion as a personal
criticism and starts taking short in-and-out breaths. These
short breaths communicate to Helen, "You're really getting to

him." If she is sensible, however, she will stop before her boss says, "Now, look here, we came here to discuss your work, not the operation of my business." Most of us face this type of confrontation at some time in our lives. Hopefully, we will listen to those breathing sounds and attempt to understand what they may mean.

*Tsk.* This sound is usually made to communicate admonishment or disgust. Marcello Mastroianni uses *tsk* as a gesture of disgust in the movie *Divorce Italian Style* when confronted with his wife, whom he despises. However, the sound can easily be misunderstood by a Syrian, since to him it means no and is used in everyday conversation. Sometimes we even hear it from a person after a sumptuous repast, when it is a teeth-cleaning exercise.

Watch out for the *tsk* sound. Do not think everything is in good order when a business associate, spouse, or friend uses the expressive sound. Except when used after a meal, you should carefully think about what a person is telling you, especially if you think the sound was uttered inadvertently.

Tightly Clenched Hands (Figure 36). In our seminars we show a video-tape recording of a negotiation in which one of

**36.  Tightly clenched hands**

the participants tenses up and clenches his hands tightly. Throughout the last portion of this recorded negotiation, the person sits with both hands clenched on the table. Of great interest is the incongruency between his verbal language and his gestural communication. For this reason it is used to illustrate how sometimes when we say things we do not mean, we are nonverbally communicating what we really feel about the situation.

In this instance the participant has cause to believe that his opposer is attempting to wipe him out in a typical "I win, you lose" negotiating situation. As a result of this feeling, he clenches his hands, stares at his opposer, silhouettes his body, crosses his legs (all gestures of suspicion), yet still manages to say weakly, "I've an open mind and want to settle this thing." His opposer senses that the verbal language is in conflict with what he perceives and does not believe what is said. This gives him false confidence and he reacts by driving even harder for a victory in the negotiation. His strategy proves to be poor, because the suspicious person's fears are increased by the augmented aggression and he withdraws further until the negotiation reaches an impasse.

At this point the negotiation was called off and the participants reviewed what had happened by watching the video-taped recording. It is not unusual during a review to have one or both of the participants acknowledge that he was totally unaware of what the other person was telling him nonverbally and did nothing positive to improve the situation. In this case, once the aggressive person became aware of his opposer's suspicious feeling toward him, he should have attempted to clear away any doubts in his opposer's mind. Instead, however, all he perceived was that there appeared to be a dichotomy between what he heard and what he sensed. He then rationalized that the other person was weak, so he attempted to pick up all the marbles but wound up with nothing.

We have observed in video tapes that people who try to

**37.  The hand-wringing gesture**

convince others while holding their hands tightly clenched do not have much success. Sometimes, when the hands are clenched, either on their lap or on a table, people rub their thumbs together or pick at the cuticle of one thumb. We believe that this gesture indicates the need of reassurance. The gesturer is uncertain and sorely needs to be made doubly sure before agreeing to resolve an issue or reach a compromise.

Wringing hands is a stepped-up version of clenched hands (Figure 37). This is observed when someone is on the hot seat, such as when being required to answer serious charges against him. After a recent local election in California the sophisticated polling equipment broke down and the registrar of voters was photographed while attempting to answer charges concerning the breakdown. As he explained his conduct, he went through the hands-wringing gesture.

Persons who have their hands tightly clenched are tense and very difficult to relate to. They should be made to relax. A technique we have sometimes used effectively is to lean toward them while talking. For example, in a superior/subordinate situation the subordinate is very suspicious of his superior's attitude. As long as his boss sits behind his desk and "looks down his nose at him," the subordinate's hands stay in a clenched position. However, when the superior gets up from behind his desk, comes around to where the subordinate is seated, and leans toward him in a gesture of confidence the hands at once come apart.

Fistlike Gestures.  Dr. Louis Loeb, in a paper entitled "The Fist," finds that this gesture communicates from the unconscious to the unconscious. His premise is that one can affect another's reaction by merely clenching the hand in a fistlike gesture and using it to emphasize the verbal language. People who clench their fists may allow them to be clearly seen, but more often they conceal the gesture by thrusting the fist in their pocket, tucking both fists under the armpits in a crossed-arms gesture, or putting both hands behind the back. Fist-clenching is essentially a masculine gesture. It is somewhat unusual to see a woman making a fist while talking.

In *Expression of Emotion in Man and Animal,* Charles Darwin observed that the clenched fist signifies determination, anger, and possible hostile action. Furthermore, he noted that a man gesturing with his fist causes an interaction that can make his opposer also clench his fist, which can result in a heated argument or other display of hostility. Albert M. Bacon wrote in *A Manual of Gestures* that the clenched hand signifies extreme emphasis, vehement declaration, fierce determination, or desperate resolve.

Primitive tribes have been known to use the fist as a gesture of defiance, and the American Indian used it in his war dances. Persons under stress tend to clench their hands, and sometimes the gesture develops into a redirected action of table-pounding

or some other physical action. It is now being used as a political identification.

Pointing Index Finger.  As a Jamaican proverb says, "A
pointing finger never says 'Look here'; it says 'Look there.'"

With few exceptions, most of us dislike having anyone point
his finger at us. We dislike it even more when we are a target
and are jabbed like a dummy in bayonet practice and asked,
"You get what I mean?" In heated arguments it is very
common to see people using their index fingers against each
other almost as épées in a fencing match. Some people use
their eyeglasses as an extension of the index finger, pointing
them in a gesture of reprimand or admonishment, or for emphasis. Since people in a quandary do not cooperate as readily
as those who are relaxed and comfortable, it behooves us not
to point our index finger at someone lest he become hostile
toward us or "turn off." Many of us have used this gesture
until it has become difficult to communicate forcefully without it. You can maintain your effectiveness and still not use
this gesture, which arouses such antagonism in others.

Politicians and clergymen would be absolutely lost without
this mannerism. They tend to use it when driving home a
point. Unlike in person-to-person intercourse, their audiences
tend not to be oversensitive to the gesture. When someone
points at a group rather than at an individual, it is always easy
to believe that the person being fingered is your neighbor,
not you. Within family groups, one finds that if the parents
use this gesture when reprimanding their children, their children may use it on their pets or dolls—a sort of pecking order
of discipline.

Anyone who has ever had a pet knows how effective the
index finger is in communicating orders or disciplining the
animal. Even though an animal may understand words, hand
signals and gestures are very effective in communicating your
wishes.

Palm to Back of Neck.  David Humphries and Christopher

**38. Defensive beating gesture**

Brannigan have recorded and analyzed (*New Scientist*, May, 1969) the palm-to-back-of-neck gesture and call it a "defensive beating posture" (Figure 38). They explain, "In more defensive situations the hand moves back, as in the defensive beating posture, but this is disguised by the palm being placed on the back of the neck." Women especially sometimes further disguise this gesture by combining it with a hair-grooming action, thinking to themselves, "He gets in my hair." When we say, "He's a pain in the neck," we are possibly verbalizing this gesture. Children under six make no attempt to disguise this beating gesture of physical aggression. In this age group the child simply raises its hand toward the head, palm of the hand facing the opponent, fingers sometimes curled but seldom clenched. Then the opponent gets belted.

You might have occasion to see this hand-to-back-of-neck gesture in your rear-view mirror the next time you are driving. If you pass another car and then cut in front of it too quickly, the driver is likely to get "hot under the collar" (Figure 39). This develops into a pain in the neck. In athletics a player or manager will sometimes take this beating posture after first removing his helmet or cap. Sometimes, not satisfied with this emotional displacement, he may throw the helmet or cap down in disgust.

Kicking at the Ground or an Imaginary Object.   When feeling angry, frustrated, or generally irritated, did you ever harbor the desire to really kick in a door? You probably have at times. Have you nonverbally communicated your emotional needs by taking a slight, restrained kicking swipe at the ground? Have you readied yourself to haul off and kick something, then held back? These are common gestures. Joe DiMaggio was a classic study of this gesture whenever he was robbed of a base hit or a home run. DiMaggio, unlike other athletes, always took a slight step-kick to show his disgust rather than the heavy-footed divot some sport figures find more suitable to their personalities. Another kicking gesture not to be confused with the disgusted action is that slight kicking action some persons use when contemplating something, or, as we say, "kicking things around."

"Turning up one's nose" describes what seems to be a universal gesture indicating dislike and rejection. Even babies instinctively "turn up their noses" at food they dislike, pulling their heads back as if to avoid an unpleasant odor. Congruent with this gesture is the downward glance described by the expression "looking down her nose at him."

**39. Hot under the collar**

Compare these frustration gesture-clusters with those under "Nervousness" in the next chapter. Try to discern the subtle differences between them.

# CHAPTER 5

# Confidence, Nervousness, Self-Control

> "Men can most always tell when a man has
> handled things for himself; and then
> they treat him as one of themselves."
> —Rudyard Kipling

## Confidence

> "The world will never learn to beware of
> these stately gentlemen who with the fixed
> calm look straight in your eyes, who never
> joke, and never waver, profuse in cautious
> hints and allusions, but practised in rightly
> placed silences—which is why the
> confidence trick is still running."
> —William Bolitho, "Twelve Against the Gods"

Confidence can bring about self-control, and the reverse is also true. Self-control can easily degenerate into nervousness and frustration. Consider all the attitudes as behavior in motion—as a *process*.

A confident person is likely to talk without hand-to-face ges-

tures like covering the mouth and nose- and head-scratching, so
in reading gestures for confidence, one should watch for a
doubt or other negative gesture that would contradict the feeling that is being projected. A proud, erect stance, often seen in
the man who has accomplished much and knows where he is
going, is also a clear indication of confidence. Perhaps that is
why we often advise youngsters to stand up straight. Not only
is it physically beneficial, but it nonverbally communicates
self-assurance. A colleague of ours goes one step further. He
claims that he can change his feelings from depression to
determination merely by squaring his shoulders and straightening his back. Confident persons have more frequent eye contact
than those who are unsure or attempting to conceal, and the
duration of contact is longer. Confidence also causes the eyes
to blink less, hence the person seems to be a better listener.

**40.  Steepling**

41. **Low steepling**

Gestures forming the clusters that communicate confidence include:

Steepling (Figure 40). This gesture is made when people join their fingertips and form what might be described as a "church steeple." Birdwhistell has used the term and we have adopted it to designate the confident and sometimes smug, pontifical, egotistic, or proud gesture. It immediately communicates that the person is very sure of what he is saying. Both Sherlock Holmes and Nero Wolfe, when explaining an "elementary" conclusion to their faithful biographers, usually assumed a steepling position to reinforce their attitude of absolute self-confidence.

There are open and covert forms of steepling. Figures 40 and 41 show the difference. Women generally use the covert,

**42. Subtle steepling**

lower-steepling gesture. They position their hands on their laps when sitting or join their fingers slightly about the belt level while standing. Clergymen, lawyers, and academicians tend to steeple often, as do business executives. Our research data indicates that the more important the executive feels he is, the higher he will hold his hands while steepling. Sometimes his hands are at the same level with his eyes and he looks at you through his hands. This is a very prevalent gesture in superior-subordinate relationships.

Several of the negotiators on our video tapes have, without being conscious of it, used this gesture as a defense when they were cornered in a weak bargaining position. In almost every instance their opposer reacted as if the person steepling had something up his sleeve and knew more than he would say. In all instances the opposer immediately changed his approach. For those who play poker, when a person is steepling, usually under the table (called "sneaky steepling"), we recommend that unless you have a very good hand, get out of the game. Of course, you must be positive that the player hasn't crossed you up with an intentionally misleading sign. We cannot possibly estimate how many persons take this posture knowingly to fool their opponents. Therefore we urge you to note the congruence of his accompanying gestures and analyze his prior and subsequent gestures before accepting the meaning of any single gesture.

A more subtle form of steepling occurs when the hands are joined more closely, the arms assuming the basic position of other steepling gestures (Figure 42). This is frequently an indication of confidence.

Hands Joined Together at the Back, Chin Thrust Upward (authority position) (Figure 43). This gesture can be ob-

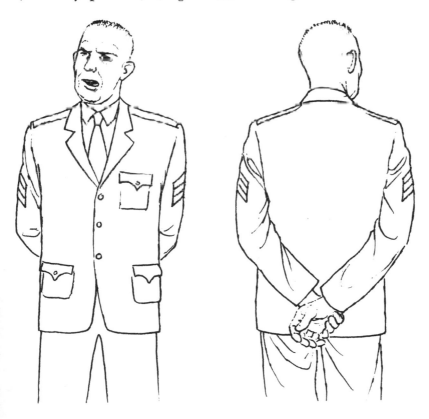

**43. Authority: the sergeant**

served in Trafalgar Square when a London bobby walks his beat, in West Germany when a customs inspector is searching baggage, or in Japan when an executive addresses his staff on the importance of the marketing plan to their firm. Many Army men recall their first glimpse of the first-sergeant swaggering out in front of a group of recruits, putting both hands behind his back and thrusting his chin forward, Mussolini-style, and possibly rocking back and forth. There was absolutely no doubt in the newcomer's mind who was in command of the situation. The verbal endorsement of these gestures may have been, "I know we have some smart college graduates out there, but I have the stripes on my arm, so that makes me boss."

But do not assume that this is only a male authority gesture. We recently observed a young female police officer in London taking the same position while walking her beat. And there are the coquettish girls who give you a shy look, drop their gaze, and put their hands behind the back, which causes their breasts to protrude. In this gesture, unlike the authority position, the hands are clenched much higher up on the back, indicating timidity. Chinese girls are admonished by their parents not to put their hands behind their back because of the provocation of protruded breasts, and the boys are told that they must accompany this position with a lowered chin, for if they do not they would appear too defiant.

Gestures Indicating Territorial Rights, Dominance, or Superiority. In *The Naked Ape* and *The Human Zoo*, Desmond Morris examines the theory of territorial rights as expressed by animals and man. He explains that male animals, when proclaiming territorial rights, either urinate or defecate, thereby signifying their boundaries. Our own observations have revealed a type of territorial-rights assertion in such actions as throwing one leg over the arm of a chair, pulling a desk drawer out and placing a foot on it, or putting a foot or feet up on a desk or chair.

**44.   Territorial rights**

Feet on Desk (Figure 44).   A national business magazine published a picture of a friend of ours in a group-management photograph. Next to him was a man with one foot on the large conference table. We jokingly said to him, "If that person on your left is not your boss, you better watch out for him." That statement got a prompt, "What the hell do you mean?" We explained that people who put their feet up on things non-verbally communicate dominance or ownership—Morris's "territorial rights." Our friend laughed and said, "Well, I guess I'm safe. That is my boss." It seems that the photographer took six pictures of the group and no feet were on the table in any of the photos. Before the seventh picture was taken, one of the group commented to the boss, "Why don't you look natural and put your feet up like you usually do?" This was the photograph that was published.

Every reader can probably go through an old family album

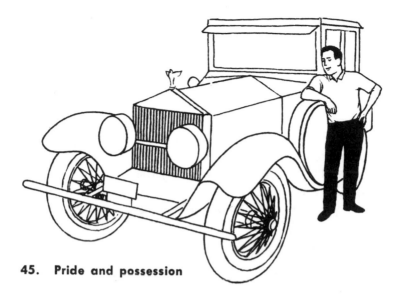

**45.   Pride and possession**

and find a relative leaning against his automobile (Figure 45). Car-owners today can still be observed touching or leaning against their vehicle while either being photographed or talking to someone about their property. They also find it difficult not to take repeated second glances at their auto when they walk away from it. Similarly, in social situations you can pick out from among couples who have been married several years those in which one partner is apprehensive about the seductiveness of the other. Nonverbally signaling rights of possession to the group, the partner may put his or her arm around the other's waist, walk hand-in-hand, or indulge in some other type of holding, letting the gesture communicate ownership or belonging.

Placing an Object on a Desired Space. Sometimes we extend our territorial rights to what Humphry Osmond has termed "sociofugal space" by distributing various personal articles —coat, purse, book, newspaper—on it, hoping it wil not be encroached upon. Students spread out their possessions when studying in a library and wishing not to have anyone near them. The theatergoer, when seats are unreserved, drapes his coat over the seat in front of him to keep others from sitting there and obstructing his view. And people entering an elevator go to different corners in much the same manner as prizefighters.

A friend of ours used to get good-looking girls to sit next to him on cross-country bus trips by taking an aisle seat—since he had observed that women like to sit by the window—placing a pillow on the window seat, then gesturing his willingness to remove the pillow every time a good-looking girl walked down the aisle looking for a seat. Giving up his territorial rights won him an enviable number of attractive companions.

Elevating Oneself. This also communicates dominance or superiority. From earliest times, gods have been depicted as dwelling on high—Valhalla or on Mount Olympus, for example. A judge sits elevated because his symbolic authority and judgment under law is final. Men and women of superior rank have been addressed as "Your *High*ness," and today we use such expressions as "look up to him," "put her on a pedestal," or "raised to the peerage." As Noah Gordon noted in *The Death Committee*, "He had climbed onto his chair and now sat on the back of it with his feet on the seat, as though on a throne looking down at them."

Whenever you wish to communicate dominance or superiority over someone, all you have to do is physically elevate yourself above him either while you are both seated or by letting him sit while you stand. Even without understanding nonverbal communication, the person will immediately get the feeling that you are "talking down to him." However, once you accept him without this elevated pretense, he may say about you, "He accepts me at his level." In our seminars we strongly urge executives not to elevate themselves or in any other way create barriers between them and their opposers. Rather, they should remove the barriers and get closer to those with whom they disagree.

Cigar-Smokers. Our research indicates that almost half of

those who smoke cigars usually associate the smoking with a special event or occasion. We have very few video-tape recordings of cigar-smokers in busines confrontations. Those that we have recorded lit up their cigars after they had achieved their objectives, never at the onset of a negotiation. We also have discovered that when a cigar is lighted, it is seldom put in an ashtray to smolder but instead is held from the time it is ignited until it is extinguished. The manner in which cigar-smokers blow out smoke is also very different from that of other smokers. They blow the smoke upward, almost as if they were about to blow smoke rings. This is especially true when the cigar-smoker feels smug or confident of his position. When he has reached this particular stage, his voice and the spacing of his puffs become deliberate.

Some believe that a motivating factor for smoking cigars is the status symbol associating cigars with wealth. In certain Latin-American countries, cigar-smoking and the *macho* concept of male virility are synonymous. Whatever the cause, we believe cigar-smokers express their confidence and self-assurance by the way they handle their cigars and blow the smoke during periods of stress.

Cluck Sound ("She was so proud she clucked like a mother hen"). When this sound is made the tongue is raised to the roof of the mouth and then released to drop quickly, making a cluck sound usually associated with a self-satisfaction gesture. Sometimes one can observe this accompanied by the snapping of the fingers and two hands meeting as if the palm of one hand were hitting a cap on a bottle held by the other. A very similar gesture is used by deaf mutes to communicate "job accomplished."

To World War II G.I.'s in Italy, the cluck sound was the same as our wolf whistle. It still communicates the same thing to a *bella* girl. Some people will cluck after tasting a good meal.

Leaning Back with Both Hands Supporting Head (Figure

**46.  Superiority**

46). A favorite cartoon of ours pictures two well-known political figures in serious conversation. Both are seated, one with his legs crossed in a figure-four position while leaning far back with both hands clasped behind his head. The other person is leaning forward with his shoulders slumped, both arms limply supported by the knees, the embodiment of dejection. When we show this at our seminar, we ask the attendees if anyone believes there is *no* communication in gestures. Very few have ever answered that no communication exists. We then ask which of the two cartoon figures is speaking and what he might be saying. The responses usually indicate that the person leaning back is in the driver's seat and that he is very sure of what he is saying. Some go further and say, "He is very smug and pedantic." The other person is described as being unhappy, dejected, doubtful, etc. In no case has anyone believed that the roles were reversed. This simple cartoon gives each person who sees it an understanding of his own awareness of nonverbal communication between persons in conflict or under stress.

Leaning back with the hands laced behind the head is essentially an American gesture, and males in the Southwest sit in this position more often than do men in other parts of the United States. Robert Markham uses this gesture to give a Western flavor to a character in *Colonel Sun:* "He laced his fingers behind his long head and leant back as far as his chair allowed, making a curious semi-Western figure in his white tee-shirt and uncoloured cotton trousers." Researching how this gesture evolved, we have found drawings in which white male settlers wearing firearms are shown sitting in this position. It might be significant that the settlers needed to draw their guns quickly. Regardless of whether this is a pistol-shooting position, a person taking it immediately communicates to you his attitude of relaxed aggressiveness. Although this gesture is mostly used by males, some women attorneys who have attended our seminars admitted taking this position when listening to a client "spill his guts." They said that the gesture allowed them greater concentration for purposes of analysis.

## Nervousness

> "Why is it that we are born into the world
> with clenched fists and leave it with
> outstretched fingers?"
> —Talmud

> "He winketh with his eyes, he speaketh with
> his feet, he teacheth with his fingers.
> Frowardness is in his heart, he deviseth
> mischief continually, he soweth discord."
> —Proverbs 6:13–14

The next time you hear someone use the hackneyed expression "He's uptight," ask him to explain why he thinks so. At first he may use the "you know" approach in an attempt to explain what he means. As a result of not being able to verbalize what he strongly feels, you may have an "uptight" person talking about another "uptight" person. We believe that he perceived an entire gesture-cluster that he labeled "uptight": A man walked into a room very rapidly and did not immediately sit down; after being asked, he finally did but chose a chair as far away as possible. Then he crossed his arms and legs and looked out the window. When asked if everything was all right, he quickly shifted his weight and position in the chair and pointed his body toward the door. From these indications, a worried, nervous, anxious condition ("uptightness") was nonverbally communicated. The receiver of this message, wondering what had caused this condition, asked, "Is everything all right?" After an unsatisfactory response, he

said, "Are you *sure* everything is all right?" This second query
caused the person to get up and pace the room rapidly before
telling the observer, "Get off my back."

Does this situation sound familiar? What has occurred is
that although the observer realized that something was wrong,
he attempted to prove it verbally and as a result alienated the
person. Sometimes the "uptight" person, feeling pressured by
the questioning, will walk out, or if he stays, he will tune out
completely. Gestures that communicate a condition of nervousness or anxiety require patience on our part because we must
wait out the other person. In his own way and time, he may
start telling us what we have already been aware of and are
waiting to hear.

The following are some gestures that form the clusters dealing with nervousness and/or anxiousness.

Clearing Throat.  Any person who has ever spoken to a
group, large or small, can remember the strange tight feeling
in his throat prior to uttering the first words. Mucus forms
in the throat due to anxiety or apprehension, so the natural
thing to do is to clear it, making that familiar sound often
heard from the speakers' podium. Some people seem to clear
their throats so frequently that one could assume that it is
nothing more than a habit. Yet many of them represent nervous
types. We can make a generalization that people who constantly clear their throats and have changes in voice inflection
and tone, signal that they are uncertain and apprehensive.

Men more so than women use this expressive sound, and
adults considerably more than children. Children may stam-
mer, stutter, say "ah," or use verbal tics like "you know," but
they are usually not throat-clearers. The conscious throat-
clearing sound made by an adult male can be a nonverbal
signal for a child or female to behave and is used as an admonishing gesture. Whatever the cause, a conscious or unconscious clearing of the throat clearly communicates a person's feelings. The world of acting has acknowledged this in
countless plays or movies with lines such as "Well, sir [clear-

ing throat], I'm really not sure of that." A playwright friend of ours in London recently had a character use this expressive sound along with the nose-touching gesture of doubt to non-verbally communicate a waiter's feeling about receiving a tip that he considered much too small.

We recommend that the next time you clear your throat you check to see if your throat itself is in any way the direct cause or if you are simply expressing apprehension about another person or about your feelings.

Whew Sound. People often use the whew sound in an air-expelling gesture—"Whew, I'm glad that's over with." Youngsters learn early to imitate adults in using the same sound and communicating the same feeling. People usually use this expressive sound when they want to communicate that some task or obstacle has been overcome. However, occasionally they are totally unaware of making the sound. They most likely are signaling the termination or easing of a somewhat doubtful situation. It is possible that the person has anxiously caught his breath and the whew sound is literally a sigh of relief.

Whistling. Our research indicates that whistling shows a variety of feelings. An interesting whistler is the warbler who makes these sounds because he is frightened or apprehensive and is trying to build up his courage or confidence. We might refer to this person as the "white-faced bird of doubt." Whenever he is in a really tight spot, he reverts to his displacement sounds for comfort. Law-enforcement authorities report that the whistle of fear varies greatly from others in prisoners' communication. These authorities believe that they can even tell by his whistle that a prisoner has been "fingered" for discipline by other prisoners.

Cigarette-Smokers. One very obvious set of mannerisms is that involving the various ways people handle their cigarettes —when lighting, smoking, or extinguishing them. Some people are more ritualistic, dignified, careful, and confident than others. Some seemingly cannot think straight without glancing at their cigarette, as though their next words were written on it. There are others who use the cigarette as a tranquilizer and take it to their lips during the intervals between periods of tension.

Our research principally concerns itself with smoking during business negotiations. Contrary to popular belief, cigarette-smokers do not smoke when extremely tense. Instead, when very tense, they either put out their cigarettes or let them burn without smoking. When we encounter doubt of this re-action at our seminars, we ask a smoker attendee what his actions might be in a real-life situation. For example, one morning shortly after he has lit a cigarette, his boss telephones and says in a very forceful tone, "Come in here right away!" Now we ask the employee-smoker to describe what he would do about smoking. He most probably will say that he would either put out the freshly lit cigarette, leave it burning in the ashtray, or go to the boss's office but put it out before entering. Once he is in the office, his boss realizes that his tone of voice has greatly upset the employee, so he quickly explains that he didn't mean to speak so harshly to him. Instead he tells him that he needs his help in solving a problem. We turn back to the smoker and ask what his actions might then be. His an-swer: "Light up."

For several years we conducted an experiment with smokers. To determine how they react when put under tension, we have them sit in a "hot seat." This consists of knowingly being video-taped and being asked questions. Next to the "hot seat" we position a large pedestal-type ashtray, which is our non-verbal way of communicating that it is all right to smoke while in that chair. However, due to the stress of sitting in front of a camera and answering seemingly innocuous ques-tions, our subject does not smoke regardless of how many packs of cigarettes he usually smokes a day. But once he has finished and returns to his original seat, he lights up. Similarly, we have observed that when a person suddenly becomes extremely tense while smoking, he tends to put out his ciga-

47.  Astonishment

rette or set it in an ashtray, where it burns until the tension is released.

Fidgeting in a Chair. We doubt if there is a single reader who at some time in his school life has not been told, "Sit still, will you?" Wouldn't it have been great to answer back, "I will, if you say something of interest to me." In a stress situation, people tend to fidget in their chairs and will continue to do so until they feel comfortable—not necessarily in the chair but with the situation.

Conducting seminars has afforded us an enormous amount of data on persons who are "fidgeters." We find that most individuals fidget for one or more of these reasons: 1) They are tired; 2) what is being said is not stimulating them to listen intently; 3) they have programmed their bodies to start responding to a specific time—say, lunchtime—and their bodies are telling them it is time for a break; 4) the chairs are not well-padded and their posteriors are complaining; 5) they are preoccupied with other things. A seminar leader who recognizes these gestures and acts accordingly is said to be able to relate to the group. A teacher is lost if he is not aware of how well his pupils are receiving his lecture material. If unresponded to, the fidgety types sometimes go into the next phase —tuning out.

Hands Covering Mouth While Speaking (Figure 47). Charles Darwin wrote that a "gesture of astonishment [is] the

hand being placed over the mouth. Sometimes this can also be
seen when one says something and is sorry or astonished at
what one said. It is almost as if we wish to shut off the flow of
words. However, they have already left our lips." Law-enforcement officers confirm our belief that the gesture communicates
emotions ranging from self-doubt to downright lying.

Many parents are familiar with this gesture when their
children react to questions about something they have done.
When the child starts to answer, the hand or hands almost
invariably come to rest somewhere in the vicinity of the
mouth. Also, if the child's hand is free and not holding anything, it will be raised to the mouth when he says, "Oops—
made a mistake." Contrast this gesture with how the child
reacts when speaking of something about which he feels enthusiastic or self-assured: Then the child supplements the
verbal language by waving, pointing, or thrusting away from
the mouth. These gesture-clusters positively endorse what is
being said rather than attempt to detract from the verbal
communication.

All of these gestures are carried into adulthood. An F.B.I.
agent recalls the bad habit he and his fellow agents had
acquired of using their hands as a shield to keep others from
overhearing while speaking to each other in public. This habit
was soon noticed by his parents and they cured him of it by
saying, "You don't have anything to hide from *us*, son, so don't
speak through your hands."

Speaking out of the side of one's mouth, a variation of this
gesture, was used in many of the movies of the 1930's to
characterize convicts or ex-convicts. Because prisoners were
then not permitted to speak to each other, talking out of the
side of their mouths was allegedly a way of circumventing the
rule. This habit supposedly stayed with them even after they
had been released from prison.

People who consciously want to hide their conversation may
also cup their hands to their mouths and speak to the listener

**48. To hide his conversation**

at an intimacy distance of from six to twelve inches. Sometimes, rather than talking through one hand, a person puts his elbows on a table or desk, forms a pyramid with his forearms, and holds both hands together directly in front of his mouth (Figure 48). He holds this position not only while talking but while listening. With very few exceptions, we have observed that such individuals were playing cat-and-mouse with their opposers until they felt it opportune to open up, at which point their hands were placed palms up or palms down on the table. The dynamics of interpersonal relations then increased, and the opposers either agreed or ended the confrontation in disagreement.

Tugging at Pants While Sitting. Pants-pulling gestures are associated with the decision-making process. It appears that when a decision is forming in a man's mind he may yank at his pants excessively while he also fidgets in his chair. After the decision is made the pants-pulling ceases. Using this man-nerism as a barometer, one is able to judge how close the other party may be to forming a decision. Much more rarely we have observed this mannerism in several men whose gesture-cluster communicated indecisiveness.

Jingling Money in Pockets.  Dr. Sandor Feldman has ob-served that people who constantly jingle money in their pocket are very much concerned with money or lack of it. Anyone who has ever visited Las Vegas gambling parlors can easily recall the ubiquitous sound of money jingling in the pockets of dice, slot-machine, or other players. One of our seminar attendees told us that the movie executive Louis B. Mayer, his personal friend, used to jingle coins constantly in his pants pocket. When he asked Mayer why he did it, the answer was, "To remind me of the time I didn't have any."

Notice how beggars have come to communicate verbally their need for money by jiggling a few coins in a tin cup. Service employees who depend on tips often seem to be pre-occupied with jingling as a means of getting their message across to their customers. Some maître d's, who would not deign to accept a coin, can be observed using the familiar gesture of rubbing the thumb on the tip of the index finger of the same hand as if feeling a bank note.

Tugging at Ear (Figure 49).  If one wants to become a good listener, one of the more difficult inclinations to over-come is the urge to interrupt. We have the capacity to listen to 650–700 words per minute, and a person speaks at a rate of 150–160. The average listener, then, has three-quarters of his listening time to evaluate, accept, reject, or contest what-ever is being said. The urge to interrupt is greatly increased whenever the speaker says something that affects the listener emotionally. At this point the listener might even gesture that he would like to interrupt and speak. One can see what difficult tasks both speaker and the listener have. If the speaker motivates the listener to a point where the listener wants

**49. Interrupt gesture**

involvement, the reception suffers because the listener now wants to change roles. If, on the other hand, the speaker emotionally triggers the listener with negative buzz words or anxiety-producing statements he runs the risk of then being tuned out and turned off. Finally, if the speaker does not motivate, involve, or in any way stimulate his listeners, his audience may fall asleep without closing its eyes. Being consciously aware of nonverbal messages is essential for eliminating some of these difficulties.

We all desire to be great conversationalists. We can achieve this if we are prepared to make the sacrifice, which is to stop talking and let another person speak when he gives his interrupt gesture. There are slightly different variations of the gesture. The grade-school custom of raising the hand as an indication of having something to say has had a lasting effect on our interrupt behavior. Although we realize that the raised-hand gesture was and still is readily recognized as a signal that we wish to speak, most of us displace it. Once the hand is raised four to six inches, it does not usually return to its original position immediately; it tends to go to the earlobe, gives a subtle pull, then returns to its starting point. Lip-suppressors, on the other hand, carry their index finger to their lips as though to seal them and stop the words from coming out. Those who restrain their interrupt gestures from touching any part of the head usually just flick their resting hand upward a few inches, then let the hand fall back. Interrupt gestures may be repeated several times without a single word being uttered. At the other extreme are those who, when they want the floor, place their hand on the speaker's forearm and physically restrain it.

Being aware of interrupt gestures and acknowledging them as signals of listener involvement do not adversely affect your message or communication. On the contrary, unless the interruption is destructive, the listener's input tells you how well you are getting through to him and the areas of his greatest resistance to your communication. When you respond to the listener's interrupt gesture he will consider you a great conversationalist because you are allowing him to participate actively in the process. As the philosopher Zeno observed, "We have two ears and one mouth that we may listen the more and talk the less."

A warning: Do not confuse a nervous ear-tugging with the more usual interrupt signal. Several persons whom we have recorded on video tape have had this mannerism and, rather than noverbally communicating that they wanted to interrupt, were signaling their nervousness and anxiety. A person giving you an interrupt gesture does not normally repeat it in rhythm as does a person who uses his ear-tugging as an outlet for his anxieties.

**50.  Self-control gesture**

## Self-Control

"The use of self-control is like the use of
brakes on a train. It is useful when you find
yourself going in the wrong direction, but
merely harmful when the direction is right."
—Bertrand Russell, "Marriage and Morals"

Patience and perseverance, we are taught at an early age,
are necessary to achieve our goals and objectives. Expressions
such as "get hold of yourself" are common. We use them as
tools to overcome frustration and keep from losing our temper.
They permit us to play a role and behave in a socially acceptable manner. People who are angry, frustrated, or otherwise apprehensive have nonetheless learned to disguise their
emotions through the use of various gesture-clusters. Holding
an arm behind the back and clenching the hand tightly while
the other hand grips the wrist or arm is one of the more
common (Figure 50), as is the locked-ankles gesture. One can
observe them on many a business or social occasion when a
person is subjected to tension, pressure, or anxiety.

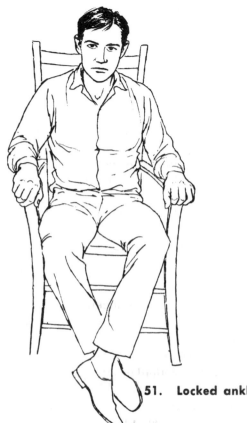

**51. Locked ankles and clenched hands**

The younger generation states that a person "shouldn't lose his cool." Unfortunately, in our change-oriented culture, older people especially sometimes find adaptation to changing values and different life-styles difficult. Staying "cool" and not losing self-control is a problem to be faced in all relationships. This type of environment provides a fertile field that gives rise to many forms of self-control gestures.

Locked Ankles and Clenched Hands (Figure 51). When we assume various locked-ankle, clenched-hands positions and ask seminar attendees to tell us what they think we might be indicating through these gestures, invariably someone will smile and say that we "look like someone who has to go to the men's room." This is quite right. These gestures designate holding back. Put yourself in a life situation. You are in the reception room of your dentist's office. Look at your feet. Are your ankles locked? If not, imagine yourself in the dentist's chair. Are they locked now? Probably. People who are holding back strong feelings and emotions assume the locked-ankle and clenched-hands position.

In a recent Army investigation of the khaki Mafia and the mismanagement of service clubs around the world, an Army colonel, when questioned under oath as to why he had not reported his findings, stated his position: There is an old Army expression about "keeping your heels locked," which means that you are not to disclose everything—the matter is not your concern.

In discussing this gesture, a friend and colleague of ours who travels by air a great deal confided that from takeoff to landing his ankles go through a continuous locking and un-locking sequence. However, when he is in his home or office he seldom locks his ankles. Admittedly, he is very apprehensive about flying. Numerous times we have recorded confrontations in which we have paid particular attention to the participant's ankles. When they were in a locked position, on video replay we asked the subject if he felt there was any relation between the gesture and the "holding back" of an offer or counteroffer. We found a high incidence of individuals who locked ankles when they were holding back a potential concession.

Airline stewardesses seem to be exceptionally able to "read" people who really want service but are somewhat shy about asking for it. Stewardesses tell us that they can spot an apprehensive traveler because he sits with locked ankles (particularly during takeoffs). This same individual may un-lock his ankles and move toward the edge of the chair when the stewardess offers coffee, tea, or milk. If the ankles stay locked, however, they sense somehow that the person who says no may really want something. The hostess then quickly

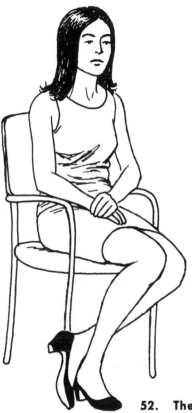

**52.    The female version of locked ankles**

responds with, "Are you sure?" This has an opening-up effect
on the passenger.

In the naturally tense situation of being interviewed for a
job, many people, both men and women, sit with their ankles
locked. Women often lock their ankles in a way that differs
from men's (Figure 52). Even when a well-known model-
training agency advised its models not to sit with their ankles
locked, too many times during an interview, when they were
uncomfortable, edgy, or dissatisfied with what was happening,
they locked their ankles in a most awkward way.

An acquaintance of ours, a dentist, assisted in our research, compiling answers to the following questions: With what frequency do men lock their ankles in the dentist's chair? How often do women lock their ankles? When ankles are locked, in what position are the hands? What type of patient sits with his ankles unlocked?

The answers showed that of 150 male patients observed, 128 sat down and immediately locked their ankles. Out of 150 women who were analyzed, only 90 initially sat in a position with ankles locked. When the ankles were locked, men tended either to clench their hands together around the pelvic area or to grip the armrests of the chair. Women also have a tendency to clench their hands but rest them on their midsection.

The individual who sits with his ankles unlocked tends to be the person who has an appointment for a routine dental check-up, which he knows will not be painful or take very long. Sometimes a person who is having extensive dental work done will become more used to the dentist's chair after four or five visits. He then does not lock ankles. Our dentist friend also revealed that when a dentist wants to use nitrous oxide gas rather than other sedatives on patients, he or his nurse always has the patient unlock his ankles before administering the gas. This is necessary, otherwise blood circulation is hampered and the gas does not have full effect. Additionally, nurses have told us that patients going into the operating room with their ankles locked and hands clenched are usually those who have not yet resigned themselves to the inevitability of the operation.

Some people try to rationalize the locked-ankle gesture by saying they feel comfortable in that position. If you are one of these, the next time you are trying to rest in a supine position and find your ankles locked, unlock them and see if you do not relax more easily.

Restraining an Arm or Gripping the Wrist. When expressing inner conflict, men as well as animals go through common and easily recognized behavior patterns. An angry man, unable to express his feelings directly, scratches his head or rubs the back of his neck in frustration. Then he may make mosaic movements (or threat postures)—clenching his fists, holding his wrist or arm, or taking a threatening step forward but remaining frozen in this hostile stance. Finally, in the redirected response, he may take out his feelings on a substitute target, a table that he bangs with a fist or a door that he kicks. These gestures are similar to those illustrated under "Frustration." These mosaic movements are gestures that we should be aware of in order to relate to or cope with the emotional states of others.

When a person assumes a threat posture we believe he is attempting to hold back a "beating" action. Therefore it is congruent that the individual will either hold the wrist of the clenched hand or restrain the entire arm by locking it behind his back. The person who restrains his arm usually does so while standing. Indeed we have yet to observe this gesture from someone in a sitting position. The gripping of the wrist, however, can be gestured while either sitting or standing. We have observed this gesture most often while the subject was seated with both arms on the table.

# CHAPTER 6

# Boredom, Acceptance, Courtship, Expectancy

> "O, what men dare do! What men
> may do! What men daily do, not
> knowing what they do."
> —Shakespeare, "Much Ado About Nothing"

## Boredom

> "We often pardon those who bore us, but never
> those whom we bore."
> —La Rochefoucauld, "Maxims"

The awareness that a listener's needs are such that you will either satisfy or bore him is often a frightening thing—a speaker gets "butterflies" and an actor gets stage fright. However, when speaking to a small group in an informal situation, we often completely forget about the two possible reactions and do a splendid job of boring our company. A person who is aware of how important it is to interest his audience, large or small, seldom forgets to look for gestures that communicate lack of interest. There are gesture-clusters that can help you discern when individuals are bored with what you are doing or saying. The rest is up to you. Either you continue to bore or you change your direction and attempt to get them interested in your ideas.

117

Drumming on Table, Tapping with Feet. The "drummer boy" who pounds his fingers in a monotonous rhythm on your desk or table is trying to tell you something about his feelings. It probably is the same thing that his counterpart, the ball-point-pen–clicker, communicates. When these two are joined by the heel-on-floor–thumper and the foot-jiggler or toe-tapper, you have a real nervous rhythm section—and the rhythm is not syncopated. Instead there is a consistent bang, bang, bang. No doubt at least one of these four has at some time irritated you by his repetitive beat. Possibly you have even been guilty of playing the role of the percussionist yourself. This is a gesture of impatience. Some psychiatrists believe that when we are impatient or anxious we try to duplicate a prior life experience when we felt safe and secure, such as when we were in the womb. At that time the mother's heartbeat was comforting. They say that we create the same type of beat to give us a feeling of security. In our impatience or anxiousness we communicate our need nonverbally by making repetitious sounds.

An associate remembers a labor negotiator called "the thumper" because of his finger-banging exercise on the nearest piece of wood. His state of mind could be easily read by his thumping and the speed-up or decrease in the tempo. When bored with the proceedings he would thump at a very fast rate, using all four fingers in series. However, when he was thoughtfully considering an offer, he merely used the middle finger in a very slight, hardly audible thump. If he was getting toward the end of his arguments and giving the offer a final look, he would pick up lint or any other foreign matter on the desk with his middle finger and study it while thumping the fingers of his other hand, almost as if to say, "Let me look at this once more." It was not until several years later, when the negotiator was no longer handling labor disputes, that he found out from his former opposer about his telltale gestures.

Head in Hand.   Among the other gestures that signal boredom is the head-in-the-palm-of-the-hand and drooping-eyes

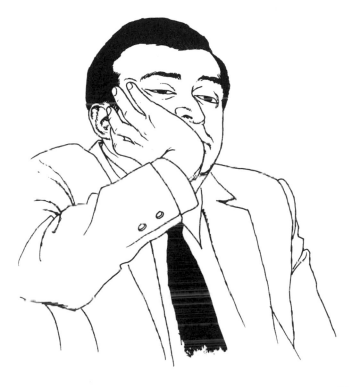

**53. Boredom**

position (Figure 53). This person does not bother to hide any feelings about what is happening. He simply puts his open hand to the side of his head in a "woe is me" gesture of regret, drops his chin in a nodding manner, and allows the eyelids to droop, half-covering his eyes.

Doodling.  Our research with business negotiators indicates that when a person doodles his interest is waning. Anything that keeps the opposers from looking at each other, like doodling, interferes with open communication, and since most doodlers tend to admire and evaluate their geometric or abstract artwork, their listening ability and consequently the communication process are jeopardized still more. The few possible exceptions we have observed to this are abstract thinkers who can carry on a conversation while their hands pursue an independent but related course, such as writing formulas. However, most businessmen tend to be concrete rather than abstract thinkers and are more aware when kept in moment-to-moment contact with the conversation.

The Blank Stare.   Another indicator of boredom is the "I'm looking at you but not listening" stare. This is a zombilike gaze coming from a person whom you may have believed was listening and now suspect is asleep with his eyes open. A sure sign that he is not interested is that his eyes hardly blink at all. Lack of blinking can indicate that the person is in a trance, asleep with his eyes open, extremely hostile, or in a deep state of indifference toward whatever is happening.

## Acceptance

> "What you are speaks so loudly that I
> cannot hear what you say."
> —Ralph Waldo Emerson

How we like people who are agreeable and willing to accept us, our ideas, and most of what we say and do! The rude awakening comes when they do not see things as we do and resist us. When this happens, rather than think that anything we said or failed to acknowledge was the cause, we believe something has basically changed in our agreeable associate.

We even have difficulty in "reading" those who are close and generally agree with us. Since we expect little opposition from them, and since they usually offer little threat to us, our awareness of their nonverbal communication can suffer. In many husband-and-wife relationships, communication breakdowns can cause difficulties, but the person responsible would be

**54. Honesty**

hard-pressed to answer such simple questions as "How do your wife's gestures tell you she is disgusted with you?" or "How does your husband signal to you that he would rather be left alone?" In a formalized culture such as prewar Japan, a wife might not indicate her displeasure with her husband verbally. Instead she might just rearrange the flowers in a vase to show her mood. The husband would know how to read this sign.

Acceptance gestures and the favorable response we get from others should be seen as endorsements of a temporary nature that, like attitudes, are subject to quick changes. One of life's most perplexing situations is confronting someone whom we had thought was agreeable who is now belligerent. Closely reading his gestures from moment to moment and not assuming that he will automatically support you is the beginning of the path to better understanding. Some of the gestures making up the acceptance cluster are as follows:

Hand to Chest (Figure 54). The hand-to-chest gesture clearly falls into the category of gestures that richly endorse

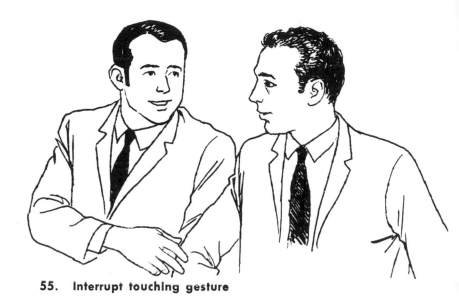

**55.  Interrupt touching gesture**

our spoken language. For centuries, man has put his hand to his chest to communicate loyalty, honesty, and devotion. The gesture goes back at least to ancient Roman times, when the Roman legions' salute of loyalty was a hand to the chest and an outward thrust of the other hand toward the person being greeted. This gesture is similar to the one used by Americans when pledging allegiance to the flag.

The field of histrionics has certainly recognized the hand-to-chest gesture, using it whenever a person is to be portrayed as sincere and honest. Pantomine experts likewise see it as meaning openness. Remember when you were a child and swore an oath or made some statement you wanted your friends to believe? Besides raising your hand with your palm exposed, you probably brought your other hand to your chest for endorsement.

We must caution, however, that, except on formal occasions, women seldom use this gesture to communicate truthfulness, dedication, or loyalty. Instead, when a woman brings one or both hands to her breasts, it is usually a protective gesture indicating sudden shock or surprise.

Touching Gestures (Figure 55). Most touchers tend to

show their emotions quickly and are particularly demonstrative toward those they like. We have observed that those who only reach out and touch another or grasp a shoulder or arm want to interrupt or emphasize a point. Others use touching as a calming gesture, usually accompanied with congruous verbal language, such as "Now, don't worry. Everything is going to be all right." But the gesture most of us enjoy is when a person we like touches us to show affection and indicate that he feels comfortable in our company.

Some researchers have interpreted the touching gesture as a need for reassurance. We do not disagree with this, since we have found that some couples attending social functions tend to touch and hold hands more as a gesture of reassurance than affection. Our only conclusion is that the touching gesture is many different things to different people—to some an endorsement, to others an interrupt signal. There are those who use it effectively to calm overly emotional persons. And many of us use it as a reassurance touch, using it not only with people we like but also with our prized possessions.

Moving Closer to Another Person. This gesture is viewed as acceptance by the individual closing the gap. He may either want to get physically closer or have some common interest to be shared in confidence. When someone becomes very enthusiastic about a topic, he often moves closer as his enthusiasm builds to a higher pitch. The difficulty in such situations is that the person being closed in on may tend to become uncomfortable and back away. He is then promptly pursued by his partner. The enthusiastic partner, in his absolute concentration on the matter at hand, often is completely unaware that the other is rejecting him and has probably turned him off. We should always be aware of how another person is reacting to our closing the distance, and the nonverbal clues he gives must dictate whether to continue or back off.

Moving toward another also nonverbally communicates to third parties that our conversation is closed to others. As an example, Joe and Hank are discussing a business problem over cocktails before a company-management dinner meeting. They are standing facing each other, toes parallel and only a short distance apart. In other words, they are standing in a closed position that makes it difficult for others to join. Although the subject being discussed is not confidential and Joe and Hank would welcome company, they are nonverbally communicating that what they are discussing is private. As a contrast, picture Howard and John standing nearby in a conversationally open position with bodies swung apart like an open hinge. This is the type of position that leads to the cocktail circle consisting of four, five, or even more persons, each contributing to the conversation.

## Courtship

> "Mingled with these groups were three or four match-making mamas, appearing to be wholly absorbed by the conversation in which they were taking part, but failing not from time to time to cast an anxious sidelong glance upon their daughters, who, remembering the maternal injunction to make the best use of their youth, had already commenced incipient flirtations in the mislaying of scarves, putting on of gloves, setting down cups, and so forth; slight matters apparently, but which may be turned to surprisingly good account by expert practitioners."
> —Charles Dickens, "The Pickwick Papers"

Dr. Albert E. Scheflen, in his article "Quasi-Courtship Behavior in Psychotherapy" (*Psychiatry*, August, 1965), discusses the elements of courtship behavior and brings out one aspect of congruence in reading gestures. He states:

> People in high courtship readiness are often unaware of it and, conversely, subjects who think they feel very active sexually often do not evidence courtship readiness at all. Courtship readiness is most clearly evidenced by a state of high muscle tone. Sagging disappears, jowling and bagginess around the eyes decrease, the torso becomes more erect, and pot-bellied slumping disappears or decreases.

We have all seen this kind of congruity (and occasionally incongruity) between couples attempting the courtship game at parties.

Preening gestures are those actions performed by the male or female, usually for the benefit of the opposite sex. After researching people's actions in situations where they wanted to look their best and convey a good first impression, we recognized that there are few people in our society who do not perform preening gestures, although the extent to which they do so varies greatly.

Despite many jokes about the unkempt appearance of hippies, they preen as much as, if not more than, a young executive decked out in a Brooks Brothers suit. Since they have more hair to contend with, they seem constantly to be smoothing it or pushing it back from their shoulders or forehead. We have found that a complete reversal takes place in the gestures of panhandlers when they wait in line at rescue missions. Instead of looking as woe-begone as possible, they tend to straighten their body, push back their shoulders, arrange their clothes, and often seem almost too proud to go in and receive a free meal.

The gestures women use to express their interest in others vary. The most common are smoothing or arranging their hair;

smoothing their dresses; turning around and looking at themselves in mirrors or glancing sideways to see their reflection. Others are a subtle rolling of the pelvic section; slow crossing and uncrossing of the legs in front of a male; and caressing the inside of the calf, knee, or thigh. The delicate balancing of a shoe on the toe of one of the feet tells a man, "You're making me feel comfortable in your presence." Should you want to test this, the next time a woman performs this gesture, say or do something you think will make her apprehensive or uncomfortable and notice how quickly she puts her shoe on. Also, some women will communicate their comfort in another's presence by sitting with one leg tucked under them (Figure 56). All of these gestures communicate a desire for involvement with another person. Couple these gestures with direct eye contact and you have a cluster indicating that the lady is definitely interested.

56–57.   Female "You make me feel so at ease" and male preening gesture.

Men also use preening gestures to communicate their interest in others. Men may straighten their ties (Figure 57), adjust cuff links, button and straighten their coats, pull up their socks when they sit down, check their fingernails, perform a cursory personal inspection of themselves before allowing an audience or person to see them. Notice the gesture-cluster a person performs when he straightens his tie, then stretches his body, thrusts his chin upward and forward—all the better to display himself to others. In observing persons in show business, you will often see this gesture-cluster performed.

## Expectancy

> "The absent have ringing in their ears when they are talked about."
> —Pliny the Elder, "Natural History"

> "An itching palm."
> —Shakespeare, "Julius Caesar"

Probably every one of us has nonverbally expressed our anticipation of receiving something and in most such instances clearly communicated our expectation—for example, by rubbing the thumb and index finger together in expectation of money. In less conscious ways we also transmit our feelings of expectation regardless of how sophisticated we may believe we are.

In many large cities, for example, doormen, bellhops, waiters, and other service employees use a variety of expectant gestures to communicate their message. The gestures range from the obvious jingling of money to what we refer to as the Egyptian stance—where the palm is turned upward in back of the body, as can be seen in ancient Egyptian art. Verbal language and pauses are a very important part of the ex-

**58. Hand-rubbing, gesture of expectation**

pectation attitude. The bellhop says, "I hope you enjoy your stay with us," then pauses and waits to see if you respond either with words or cash. Or the maître d' states, "Mr. Smith, let's see if we have a nice table for your party." Overlooking these cues can result in your receiving commensurate service.

Rubbing of the Palms (Figure 58). When a youngster sees his mother pull up in a station wagon filled with goodies from the supermarket, he is very likely to rub his palms together as a gesture of expectation. Or take a sixty-year-old company president who is conducting a very important executive meeting when his secretary brings in a message. He gets up from his chair after reading it, rubs his palms together, and says, "Men, we got that big XYZ contract." We recall a person with a poor reputation for business ethics who was often described as having "both hands out and itchy palms."

Could this mean that itchy palms should be rubbed as a gesture of expecting to receive something?

During one of our recorded negotiation sessions a participant unexpectedly rubbed his hands together rapidly, gesturing that he expected something. We were very surprised to see this gesture at the start of the negotiating. We stopped the program at this point and inquired if there had been any prearranged plan between the negotiators. Their smiles told us we had indeed uncovered a situation in which the two had reached a prior agreement and were going through the motions to convince us that they were extremely good actors as well as negotiators. His motion of rubbing his hands only convinced us that he knew and liked what was coming. Often people rub their hands together in a washing motion prior to undertaking an activity. Unless their hands are cold, they are probably nonverbally communicating their intense interest in that activity. Maybe that is why many crapshooters rub the dice between their hands before rolling them.

Another gesture, not as spirited or obvious, is slowly rubbing wet palms against a fabric. Rather than conveying expected confidence, the gesture seems to communicate nervousness. Many people who are unsure of themselves and nervous will slowly dry their sweaty palms on something. Men usually use their trousers, whereas women usually use a handkerchief or tissue. Many people under stress, such as witnesses testifying in court, a novice making a speech, or athletes awaiting the start of a race or game, perform some sort of palm-sweat–removal gesture.

Crossed Fingers. A gesture that probably is a throwback to when we were children is the act of crossing the middle finger over the index finger. The gesture is frequently accompanied by the incantation "I cross my fingers and hope to die, if you ever catch me in another lie." Dr. Sandor Feldman in *Mannerisms of Speech and Gesture* states that this is "a magic gesture, a defense against evil, whether that evil comes from within ourselves or from outside." Although adults usually use it as a figure of speech, sometimes the gesture accompanies the spoken word. As an example, during a plane trip one passenger, referring to an airplane connection in a large city noted for long delays in landings, crossed his fingers and said to another, "If you cross your fingers, you just might make it." Remember also that youngsters cross their fingers not only when telling a "little white lie" but also when hoping for good luck. In this situation, as Dr. Feldman states, it is done to avert evil.

But how often do adults in business or social situations perform this gesture—consciously or unconsciously? More often than is realized. The adult gesture is usually a very subtle one with the fingers quickly crossed and then uncrossed. The crossed-finger gesture has been recorded in many tense situations where an individual has made a request or demand and then slightly crossed his fingers signifying that he hoped his wishes would be granted. In some Latin-American countries the crossed-finger gesture is consciously used to signify that two people are very close to each other. In the United States the gesture of two fingers held together but not crossed might accompany a statement such as "We're as close as that."

# CHAPTER 7

# Relations and Circumstances

*"Circumstances are beyond the control of man; but his conduct is in his power."*
—Benjamin Disraeli, "Contarini Fleming"

Nonverbal meaning can change depending on where, when, who, and how. We are now going to subject gesture-clusters and attitudes to life situations. Deeper appreciation and meaning can result from seeing the gesture-clusters and attitudes take shape in operational situations. In this chapter we will deal primarily with relationships. In the following chapter, with some guidance, you will be taken through day-to-day experiences.

## Parent and Child

Oh, what a tangled web do parents weave
when they think that their children are naive.
—Ogden Nash, "What Makes the Sky Blue"

Mothers are said to be much more responsive and aware of their children's needs than are fathers. As Victor Hugo observed, "Men have sight, women insight." After all, the mother has had to respond more so than the father to nonverbal communications from her offspring during its first two years, before any verbal communication was possible. As a result of this experience she senses much more accurately how her children feel.

Sound and decibel level are often modes of nonverbal communication in the parent-child relationship. Messages are conveyed by such things as slamming doors, playing music loud, and screaming. In addition, it is usually agreed that a mother can tell whether a child's crying indicates that it wants food, needs a change, is sick, or perhaps just tired. However, various experiments have shown that a mother cannot recognize messages solely on the basis of her child's cry. These tests consisted of tape recordings of the various cries of the child presented to the mother for identification while she was isolated from her child. Under these circumstances the mother could not distinguish one cry from another. This, however, is not difficult to understand. We should not expect a mother to do better than any other person trying to receive a message when that message is limited to a single word, sound, or gesture. The mother's ability depends upon the gesture-cluster, the congruity of the message, and the circumstances involving the cry. All of these communication devices are used by her to understand and satisfy the child's needs.

Later, in adolescence, the mother can know how her child feels by the way he sings, whistles, hums, plays the radio, or engages in other sound-producing activities. Sometimes her feelings may be the complete opposite of her husband's. An example of this is the different meaning each attaches to door-slamming, as when a child leaves the house to go to play as contrasted with when he leaves the house after a particularly unrewarding confrontation with his parents. Many fathers tend to put all door-slamming in one category, whereas mothers see different types.

In our research, almost all parents commented that the gestures their children gave when trying to hide something were the most obvious. Without exception, each parent stated, "I know when my child is lying or trying to cover up something." What was very difficult for them was trying to describe *what* it was in terms of gestures, noise, or facial expressions. The most common mannerisms mentioned were: not looking at the parent, blinking rapidly, covering their mouth when speaking, twitching, looking down, shrugging shoulders, swallowing repeatedly, wetting their lips, constantly clearing their throat, rubbing their nose, scratching their head while talking, putting their hand to their throat, and rubbing the back of their neck.

Reversing our research, we asked many children who the person was that they had the most trouble lying to, and they unanimously responded that their parents were. When asked who the easiest person to lie to was, they said the grandparents.

## Lovers

In a roomful of people, can you tell which ones are married and which are not, which ones have a strong lover's bond and which do not; which ones are uncomfortable with each other and which are not; and which couples would rather be home in each other's company and which would not?

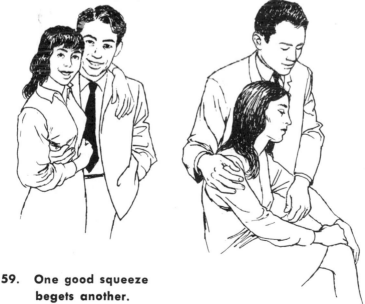

**59. One good squeeze begets another.**

**60. No need for words**

**61.  The stare, the touch**

Love suits some people well and others badly. We have observed that with those to whom it is meaningful, certain mannerisms and gestures occur that are peculiar to them (Figures 59–61).

In a group, married women rather than unmarried tend to pair off with another woman, and unmarried women tend to pair off with men. Very seldom does one observe two single women conversing, and if one does, the conversation is short-lived.

Unmarried couples tend to stay together through most of the evening, almost as if to signal to the group that they belong together. Couples who have had a quarrel and are attending the function despite the strained relations tend to be very formal toward each other. If smiling at each other, it is a contrived smile with no teeth showing. Generally, a married or single couple who are not on the best terms do not touch each other very often, and when one does the other responds by quickly withdrawing the hand or arm touched.

As we have mentioned before, touching shows rights of possession and is a gesture of assurance or reassurance. The sender may be reassuring the receiver, understanding the receiver's need for assurance. Where the parties are on good terms, one good squeeze begets another. In studies of primates it was found that touching gestures were nonaggressive and calming. Lawrence K. Frank in his paper "Tactile Communication" (*ETC.*, 1958) shows the importance of tactile experiences in personality development. He found that our needs differ, based upon the way they were satisfied in infancy. It is in adolescence and during periods of loving that we see an increase in frequency of tactile communication. It is easy to recognize that very strong aspects of the love relationship are the touching gestures and the need to be touched.

Albert Scheflen has observed that individuals assume positions for courtship, such as positioning their chairs and leaning toward each other and sometimes placing their chairs or extremities in such a way as to block out others. Besides the preening and positioning for courtship, Scheflen found that there appeared to be actions appealing for or inviting courtship. These invitations are usually flirtatious glances, gaze-holding, demure gestures, head-cocking, and rolling of the pelvis. In women he observed crossing of legs, a slight exposure of the thigh, placing a hand on the hip and exhibiting the wrist or palm, protruding the breast, and slow stroking motions of the fingers on the thigh or wrist.

## Strangers

> **"I do desire we be better strangers."**
> **—Shakespeare, "As You Like It"**

Erving Goffman made an interesting observation in *Behavior in Public Places:* "One might say as a general rule that acquainted persons in a social situation require a reason *not* to enter into a face engagement with each other, while unacquainted persons require a reason to do so."

A determining factor in the amount of nonverbal commu-

nication between strangers is whether one or the other is
considering any involvement. As an example, two strangers
boarding a subway at the same time late in the evening may be
very apprehensive about each other and decide not to make
any eye contact. As we have said, eye contact means recogni-
tion, which sometimes precedes conversation and involvement.
By not exchanging glances these two travelers are communicating a lack of interest in each other, even though they share
an uneasy feeling about the situation.

If, on the other hand, one wants to gain reassurance he
might display a gesture-cluster of first looking at the other
person, clearing his throat or blinking, then saying something
noncontroversial like "Subways are not very crowded this late
at night" or "Seems strange not to get pushed around by a
mob." Depending on the level of uncertainty each feels concerning the other, their ages, their sex, and their respective
attitudes about engaging in a conversation, this situation could
produce anything from a suspicious look to an interesting and
provocative conversation that might even lead to a more
permanent relationship.

We have found that different opening nonverbal signals are
used in various cities. Understanding the fact that there are
differences can keep one out of some rather embarrassing
situations. Recently, while flying from Atlanta to New York,
we encountered this factor in a discussion with a very gracious
Southern lady. It seems that she disliked going to New York
City because of the indifference that people displayed toward
others. "Moreover," she said, "I don't especially enjoy not being
looked at and being made to feel that I don't exist. Why, in the
South we take the time to look at people and, as you know,
smile at them." (Indeed it has been observed that Peachtree
Street in Atlanta is a location where one is smiled at very
often.) After the lady had explained her disappointment with

what she termed the "unfriendliness" of people in New York City, we explained that individuals' nonverbal signals vary from city to city, section to section, and country to country.

In densely populated areas such as in New York City and Tokyo, people give the impression that they are disregarding one another. A newcomer might take their gestures to mean complete indifference. Yet studies conducted to determine how people in crowded cities react during a time of crisis—such as the 1965 New York power blackout—reveal that an overwhelming majority respond by helping others in need. These "good Samaritans" with hard-shell exteriors show their true colors at such times. In less densely populated areas where individuals depend on each other more and Western or Southern "hospitality" prevails, signals such as smiles, winks, and a warm "Howdy" are commonplace. A New Yorker, however, would probably be taken aback if greeted in this manner by a stranger.

The gestures of people at a bar are interesting to observe. The location of the bar is significant. If the bar happens to be at an airport, the scene is similar to that of a subway during rush hour. There is the same mad dash and the lack of eye contact, generally creating a picture of people lost in their thoughts and oblivious to their surroundings. Aware of this, the bartender pours drinks and rings up sales like a person interested only in performing his functions rather than becoming involved with his customers.

At a hotel bar there is often at least one man who takes what we call a "hunter's position." This fellow usually sits at the curve of the bar and evaluates the prospects as they parade before him. All of the action is either directly in front of him or to his side, so he can use his eyes to maximum effect. The shy person, on the other hand, keeps track of what is going on in the bar by furtive glances in the mirror.

The male hunter's counterpart is the woman who stations herself so that her field of vision is not interrupted. If she is attractive, however, she has a handicap, for men will offer to buy her a drink. When this happens she must turn down the offer and still communicate that she is interested in the *right* person. Sometimes she does this by rejecting the overture and at the same time giving the person of her choice some sign, a look perhaps that says, "You're the one."

## Superior and Subordinate

"A load of cares lies like a weight of guilt
upon the mind: so that a man of business
often has all the air, the distraction and
restlessness and hurry of feeling of a criminal."
—William Hazlitt

What some have referred to as the authority of territorial-rights gestures predominates in many superior/subordinate relationships. The more aggressive the superior is when the subordinate feels threatened or insecure, the more exaggerated their gestural roles are likely to be. A degenerating chain reaction then occurs; it becomes a "can you top this" encounter from which neither can retreat and which neither can win. They both will probably lose because their needs are not being satisfied, much less recognized

Superiority can be expressed in the initial handshake. When someone grabs your hand firmly and turns it over so that his palm is directly on top of yours, he is attempting a type of physical domination. When a person offers you his hand with the palm up, he is showing a willingness to accept a subordinate role.

A seminar attendee once stated that it had never occurred to him how important it was "not to stand or tower over another person when he is seated, because it tends to make others feel small in your presence and seems nonverbally to communicate a superiority in your position." He had found out the hard way that many people resent another person's taking such a position. The feet-on-the-desk gesture is also often found in superior/subordinate situations. When this gesture is used, the reaction toward this pompous position of authority by those who do *not* have their feet on the table is usually negative. A subordinate generally resents it; a superior will not tolerate it; but an equal may be indifferent to it.

In many superior/subordinate relationships, especially if they have existed a long time, facial expressions tend to predominate over body gestures. An example is the raised eyebrows, the slight twisting of the head, and the look of doubt a boss gives when he does not accept his subordinate's "make-a-million idea." Or he may avoid eye contact, thereby unconsciously communicating that he is through with the subordinate for the moment. If the subordinate is not alert and does not pick up the signal, then he may have to resort to stage two—shifting his weight, possibly giving a large sigh while glancing at his watch. If for some reason the message still does not get through, he may stand up or pick up his papers as if to stuff them away and then ask bluntly if the subordinate does not have some other business to attend to or, more diplomatically, advise him that he just has time to make another appointment. Hopefully, an aware person need not be taken this far. Bluntness can cause loss of respect for both parties. The superior wonders how dense his employee must be not to recognize the clearly sent gestures, and the subordinate leaves with a feeling of having been made a fool of by his boss and yet angry with himself for not having recognized the signals that he had outlasted his welcome.

**62.  Preoccupation**

Figure 62 shows an executive clearly preoccupied with many problems. If, as you entered his office, you were to see your boss in this position, your first feeling might very well be to leave him alone, especially if what you had wanted to speak to him about was a serious matter. Reading his gestures, you might decide to wait before alerting him to more problems. Such awareness is a valuable asset in furthering your career.

A seminar attendee reported, "We have a boss who turns his staff off completely by putting his feet on the desk while rambling on about topics having nothing to do with business and then doesn't pick up any of the cues we send him which communicate that we have work to do and would like very much to do it." In superior/subordinate relationships a great deal of time is wasted primarily because either the boss or the employee is so absorbed in what he wants that he is not concentrating—not open to the gestural communication that tells him it is time to turn off and leave.

In Figure 63 the standing man is the superior. His overall posture is more relaxed than that of the seated man. He is standing in a dominant position—almost in back of the desk, thereby trespassing on the subordinate's territory. His hand is casually inserted in his coat pocket with the thumb sticking out, another gesture of confidence and authority that is common in Europe and the United States. We have recorded this gesture many times with the subjects both seated and standing. Often, when two people who characteristically take this position meet, they refrain from using the gesture in defer-

**63. A superior/subordinate relationship. Which is which?**

ence to the other. In Figure 64 the speaker is the superior telling his men, "Last year's operation was not up to our standards" and that they had better improve or else. His clenched fist indicates authority, and he is either emphasizing a point or threatening an unpleasant course of action. The speaker is also attempting to show his dominance by standing while giving his executives a dressing down. Also note that each man has his coat buttoned and a grim look on his face.

Figure 65 shows another superior/subordinate relationship. In A the boss is beckoning to an employee that he wants to see him. In B the boss is in the process of admonishing or threatening the employee with his index finger while the employee stands in a position of readiness, hands on hips. The employee reacts to abuse and aggressively puts his hands on the desk, leans forward, and tells the boss how he feels about the situation (C). The boss has withdrawn from his posture

**64.   The day of reckoning**

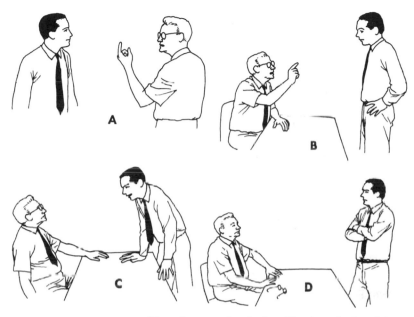

**65. A superior/subordinate relationship**

in B as a result of the employee's outburst. In D the employee, after getting his time at bat, assumes a defensive gesture with arms crossed. The situation having degenerated, the boss removes his glasses, puts his hands on the table, and is ready to dismiss the employee.

## Client and Professional

> "The best client is a scared millionaire."
> —Quoted by H. L. Mencken

The client/professional relationship is a sensitive one, with more than the usual interpersonal problems. Most professionals —lawyers, accountants, consultants—readily admit that their ability to communicate with a client could be improved. But let us look at the relationship from the client's point of view.

A prevalent attitude held by clients is "This is my unique problem. Show me something new." The client sincerely wishes to believe in the professional's expertise yet does not trust a technique that may have been used before. As a result an initial suggestion of a possible direction to take is often disregarded.

Then, too, since the client has probably spent considerable time attempting to solve his problems—which worry has increased in number and complexity—he does not expect or want a simple solution, even though to one who is not involved the solution may seem the best to be found at that time. The client also usually needs empathy from the professional, since he believes that only someone that has a "feel" for his problem can help him. If he does not experience this empathy, the client often believes the professional has lost his touch with people.

Some clients only hear what they want to hear, in which case the professional acts merely as an amplifier of the client's uninformed thoughts. He sometimes wants a devil's advocate to argue against any sound approach to his real or imagined problems. Some clients seem to believe that the expert possesses supernatural powers and that with the wave of a magic wand all his troubles will vanish. Sometimes clients believe that a person with a different point of view can help, or they want to be soundly criticized and put back together in a form that is stronger than the original. This desire for self-discovery through the help of others might explain the tremendous interest in encounter groups and sensitivity sessions. A "completely open" type of revelation is desired, in which the person hopes to discover himself and how he affects others. In this type of exchange, the professional is sometimes faced with the dilemma of how to best communicate his conclusions to the client.

What are the gestures in a client/professional relationship? What causes the client concern and what turns him on? A most conspicuous, supposedly relevant, gesture on the professional's part is taking notes of what the client is saying regardless of whether he attaches any importance to it. Another is the hand-to-face evaluation gesture, the thinker-type posture that many professionals almost automatically assume when a problem is presented by them. This is an important gesture and one that creates a feeling of confidence in the client. It shows that the expert is not only interested but has already started to analyze the client's predicament. There is, however, a situation in which this gesture is awkward—when two pros use it on each other. Instead of getting a positive response, each pro believes the other is being "picky" and critical of what he is saying.

In a recent TV special involving the problems confronting the courts, two attorneys appeared to completely turn each other off not by what was said but by their gestures. Had they used the same gesture with a client, it probably would have been effective; however, with another lawyer, it seemed to be interpreted as doubt, thereby causing them difficulties in communicating with each other. When two professionals take the open "Lincolnesque" position (Figure 66), they are much more agreeable and tend to resist each other less, as they probably do not feel threatened from a professional point of view. Many professionals still do not consider that there is a difference between dealing with a client and dealing with an associate. By using inappropriate gestures they inadvertently send misleading communications.

Leaning forward toward the client is a gesture of interest. However, too often we have observed the professional sitting back in his chair with an aloof steepling gesture that can almost indicate indifference toward the client's problem. In addition, the professional might be seated behind a large desk

**66. Two professionals in Lincolnesque position**

that serves as a barrier to his client, who cannot be blamed for thinking, "He is not on my side. He doesn't care about my problems, only about the money he can make." This is contrary to the fact that most professionals are very dedicated men and *do* care. To combat this impression an increasing number of them are rearranging their offices in order to achieve a more personal atmosphere, one in which stronger ties are established with their client and fewer adverse emotions are created before the problems and possible solutions are discussed.

The professional should not communicate dominance or adopt a pedantic attitude toward his client. In a situation where the client behaves like a lost child, it is very easy to be a judge, father, and big brother to him. Not only do such gestures as holding the lapels of the coat make this attitude evident to the client but it is reinforced by verbal language in such expressions as "Do you follow me?" or "Is that clearly understood?"

Some professionals feel as though they have to *sell* their capability. In most cases, however, the client probably has already checked his reputation before ever contacting him. Therefore, except in rare instances, little or no selling should be required. Instead, a good listening attitude should prevail in an effort to find out what the client's problems and needs are.

Recently a prospective client faced with a complex negotiation contacted us and requested a meeting to outline his requirements. When the meeting started he "qualified" us—he wanted to know what our credentials were in the field of contractual negotiations with government agencies. After we stated that we had such experience, he tried to evaluate our involvement and results. Very quickly we sensed—verbally and nonverbally—that the client needed additional reassurance. Prompted by this awareness, we asked him how he happened to hear about us. He then reported what others had said about us. In so doing he gave himself the reassurance he needed. Once over this, we proceeded to the main purpose of the meeting—our client's needs. If we had not seen our client initially sit back, cross his arms in a "show me" attitude, and nonverbally communicate that he was not convinced, we might have attempted to "sell" him when he was not prepared to buy. Instead we deferred to his initial judgment in seeking our counsel and let him convince himself of our capability. Awareness of the client's attitude and emotional concern as communicated by his gestures can make the professional/client relationship an extremely satisfying experience for both parties.

## Buyer and Seller

Many professional salesmen and buyers with whom we have discussed nonverbal communication have stated that they could tell at once when something was wrong by the way a customer or vendor walked into the office and sat down. It is not until we have discussed the details in depth that they begin to see how much they already know about interpreting gestures.

In many typical sales transactions both parties adopt the "I am going to win and you are going to lose" attitude. This causes an elevation of emotional reactions. Let us outline such a situation.

The buyer sits back, away from the desk, folds his arms, crosses his legs, and suspiciously says, "What do you want to talk about?" The seller might respond by getting up on the edge of his chair, feet in a sprinter's position, body leaning forward in a take-charge attitude, waving his hands and using his index finger to drive home his point. The seller's initial gestural advances can cause the buyer to become suspicious, especially if he is one of those who bitterly resent a hard sell. The "Tell you what I'm going to do" approach causes the buyer to withdraw and become defensive.

Instead of changing to an alternate plan, or motivating the buyer to get involved, the seller now becomes insecure because his ideas are not accepted. At this point the seller's gestures tend to be defensive. He may push himself away from the desk, twist his body in a silhouette, cross his legs and arms, then ask such ineffective questions as "What's the matter with you? Don't you understand?" or "Why are you being so unreasonable?" This line of questioning only serves to drive the two further apart.

When this stage is reached there are very few instances where either a buyer or a seller is expert enough to restructure or wind down the emotions in order to solve their problem or reach an agreement. A "Let's call it off or postpone it" attitude prevails. Often the atmosphere becomes so negatively charged that each side starts accusing the other of causing the breakdown. In day-to-day situations this is the point where we rationalize that "It was the other guy's fault we didn't

**67. The purchasing agent as seen by a salesman**

settle. How can we do business with people like that?"

Those executives attending our video-taped practice seminars, however, have a second chance. We can replay what took place and objectively review why and how the negotiation failed. Being able to see and hear their mistakes gives each participant a greater insight into a degenerating process that they can avoid in future life situations.

Some businessmen, both buyers and sellers, believe that once they have been exposed to this form of training-by-viewing, they have an overwhelming advantage over their opposers. But this is not completely true. All they have is a better understanding of the attitudes and emotions that are being communicated by their opposers. They still must develop their ability to read congruency of gestures, to evaluate by testing, and, most important, to understand how they themselves are responding to gestures. The phrase "putting it all together" probably best explains what we hope may happen.

To young, inexperienced salesmen many purchasing agents are ogres like the one in Figure 67. And some purchasing agents assume this characteristic pose because they like to have others squirm, talk too much, or simply perform while they themselves act as spectators rather than participants. A hard man to sell? Yes indeed! But if the salesman can get him involved by asking questions that deal with his needs, the glacial attitude may melt. If not, the buyer's next gesture may be to put down his glasses ("That's it! Get out"), cross his arms ("Your time is running out"), or begin to shuffle papers ("I've got more important things to do").

Experienced salesmen know how important it is to "close the gap" between buyer and seller, so they usually manage to have available photographs, reports, or other visual presentations. With these they try to move around the desk, either to the same side as the buyer or at a right angle to him. If the buyer reacts to the salesman moving closer by crossing his arms or making some other defensive gesture, this communicates his displeasure. The salesman should take care to return to his original position on the opposite side of the desk. Some people are extremely sensitive about their position of dominance behind a desk and will fight to maintain their image.

**68.   Buyer and seller**

Figure 68 presents gesture-clusters that might be seen in a typical buyer/seller relationship. The buyer is leaning far back in his chair, away from the seller, and is steepling. His coat is buttoned and his legs are crossed while he swings one foot as if impatient with what is being said. A slight scowl indicates he is not ready to buy or accept what the seller is offering. The seller is leaning forward in an action-oriented position. His gesture with the upturned palms of his hands, his simple smile, and unbuttoned coat indicate he is being open and desires the buyer to feel comfortable. He has reached the critical stage of his sales presentation. If he says the wrong thing now, the buyer may signal this by crossing his arms over his chest or recrossing his legs so that the elevated foot points away from the seller and toward the nearest exit.

# CHAPTER 8

# Understanding
# in an Environment

We are ready for final immersion, understanding the media. The following are a few typical life situations, some familiar, some strange, but all designated to help you test and realize your nonverbal quotient.

## Gestures without an Audience: Telephoning

We gesture regardless of whether we have an audience. At no time is this more apparent than when you are on the telephone. Have you ever noticed the cord on your telephone receiver? It is probably twisted. Whether you are left- or right-handed you tend to shift the phone from hand to hand in order to gesture. Observe how much you gesture and how much more frequent the gestures are when the conversation tends to be exciting, frustrating, enthusiastic, or in other ways interesting.

In your observations at the airport in Chapter 1 you saw three different callers portraying three different gesture-clusters and attitudes (Figures 1–3). Here are some of the other gestures people use while phoning.

Doodling.  There are probably very few of us who cannot identify with the person who writes words or numbers, draws lines or circles, or whatever while on the telephone. Abstract thinkers can make symbolic representations and not be distracted from the conversation. But concrete thinkers, a category that includes most of us, tend to doodle when they are uninterested in the conversation.

Smokers' Gestures. Very seldom does a smoker who is involved in an interesting conversation hold his cigarette, pipe, or cigar while talking or listening. Instead he sets it aside and comes back to it. But if he becomes angry or disturbed, he will pick up what he's smoking and flick the ashes, and if he's really upset, he'll grind it out in a gesture of extreme hostility.

Preening Gestures. Male and female gestures of courtship are in full bloom during telephone conversations. Straightening the tie, adjusting clothing, and arranging hair are common. One gesture that occurs only while telephoning is the woman's looking at herself in the mirror as she talks to her boyfriend.

Rocking or Swinging in Chair. An executive whom we know rocks his chair either forward and backward or from side to side while talking on the telephone. He usually does this when he feels very much in control of a situation and is confident things will work out in his favor. Once this self-satisfaction is interrupted, his gestures change abruptly. He stops the rocking, swinging movements, clenches a fist, and picks things up and puts them down with force.

Feet on Desk. Those who feel dominant or confident of themselves in the presence of others may assume this position even while telephoning.

Pulling Out Bottom Desk Drawer to Use as Footrest. This gesture usually indicates "getting a leg up" on someone or some situation. Indeed many aggressive, goal-oriented executives seem to confront problems with a great deal of gusto while gesturing in this manner while on the telephone.

Opening and Closing Top Desk Drawer. There is an executive who pulls his top drawer out and then pushes it in whenever he is on the telephone and confronted with a complex problem. He may do it many times. This is his meditating gesture. When he has reached a solution he shuts the drawer, stands up, and delivers his answer in a firm tone.

Standing Up. Of all telephone gestures, this is probably the most common. We do stand up a great deal when talking on the telephone—considerably more than most of us think. We tend to stand up while making decisions, when surprised or shocked, and when restless and bored with the conversation. Other gestures in the cluster will provide clues about which emotion is involved.

Watching one side of a phone conversation can supply much more information than the person on the other end of the line ever receives.

## The Courtroom

"Trust not a man's words if you please, or
you may come to very erroneous conclusions;
but at all times place implicit confidence in
a man's countenance in which there is no
deceit and of necessity there can be none."
—George Borrow

Everything that is said in a court of record is transcribed, and if an error has been committed by the judge or one of the lawyers, it can be the subject matter raised on appeal. Lawyers and judges have long realized that there are many types of nonverbal communication that can express their true feelings and are not taken down.

One criminal-court judge would charge the jury in different ways, depending upon whether he thought the defendant was guilty or innocent. He would stand when he came to those sections of the charge that were favorable to a defendant whom he thought was innocent. But if he thought the defendant was guilty he would stand to emphasize those sections most damaging to the defendant. Needless to say, the standing or seated position of the judge (whom court officials referred to as the judge with the standing charge) was not transcribed by the court stenographer.

**69.  The cock of the walk      70.  The Rock of Gibraltar**

Many successful attorneys use their awareness of nonverbal communciation to evaluate their colleagues, witnesses, and members of the jury. Judge James C. Adkins (*Trial Magazine,* December/January, 1968–69) states that in jury selection some lawyers consciously evaluate gestures that communicate an individual's characteristics and attitudes. Albert S. Osborn in his study, "The Mind of the Juror," also suggests that certain gestures, particularly those around the mouth, are very revealing. Louis S. Katz (*Trial Magazine,* December/January, 1968–69) states, "If a prospective juror keeps his fists clenched when questioned on qualifying by one attorney and spreads his hands out when the other attorney·is talking, the first lawyer had better not keep that juror." Katz further believes that hands nonverbally communicate whether the juror or potential juror is open-minded, hostile, or prosecution-minded. Jury members themselves, perhaps less conscious than lawyers of the implications contained in gestures, still rely on them to some degree in appraising the evidence in a case.

The gesture shown in Figure 69 says, "Humble as I am, your honor . . ." but it is not limited to courtroom use. Other professions besides the legal have their own lapel-holders. If vest pockets are handy, they may even tuck their thumbs in them while clinging to the coat lapels.

"Go ahead and throw whatever you will at me—I won't budge" is clearly expressed by the posture and facial expression of the witness in Figure 70. One of the attorneys and perhaps both of them will have great difficulty in getting him to open up and reveal his emotions.

Figure 71 illustrates a typical courtroom scene. The lawyer

**71. Attorneys and potential jurors**
Juror #1. Fists clenched, arms crossed, legs crossed European style. Examining attorney should not accept him. Juror #2. Steepling, leaning back, legs not crossed. Test further for reason of confidence. Juror #3. Hands on rail, leaning forward, head tilted. Accept him. Juror #4. Hands clenched in front of stomach, legs crossed European style. Test with further questions to find out why he needs self-control. Juror #5. Leaning back with hands supporting back of head, legs crossed. Question further to make him reveal the conclusion of his evaluation. Juror #6. Hand on thigh in readiness posture. He could take leadership of the jury. Direct comments and glances at him in order to win him over to your side. Finally, the attorney on the right, with hands on hips and coat unbuttoned in a gesture of openness, is more appropriate for examining the jurors. The other attorney has taken a pompous stance, which may turn the jury against him.

standing before the potential jury is asking them questions and deciding which ones he will permit to remain on the panel and which he will excuse. You do not have to be a lawyer to make the following judgments: Without looking at the captions, determine why you would 1) reject a juror, 2) accept a juror, 3) continue to question him. Finally, which attorney's stance is more appropriate for the examination of the jurors?

## Social Gatherings

"Man seeketh in society comfort, use, and protection."
—Francis Bacon, "The Advancement of Learning"

Many times it can be as much fun watching people at a party as being a participant. A great deal of our pleasure comes from watching the nonverbal communication that is taking place. Courtship gesture-clusters are always in evidence at parties, but other drives and needs are present and just as fascinating to observe as the more flamboyant, sexually motivated behavior. Figure 72 gives three party-group interactions.

The two men standing in the center are probably discussing something unimportant and by their "open" stance are inviting others to join them in their conversation. Notice that both have their coats unbuttoned, are friendly toward each other, and that one has his thumb tucked under his belt. He also is standing confidently with legs spread apart. The other man has his hands resting at his side with fingers relaxed. Both are leaning slightly toward the other. The two women on the right are seated and looking at the two standing men. One of them is leaning toward the other and is approximately twelve inches away while telling her companion something that is probably very confidential. One could suspect whom they are talking about. Both women have their legs crossed. Their hands are

72. Social gathering showing acceptance/courtship, openness, and secretiveness

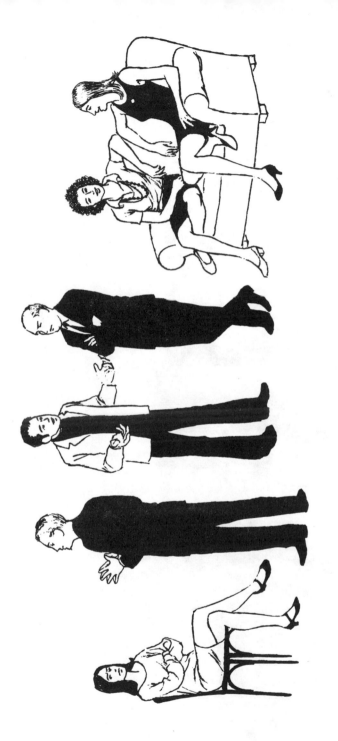

73. Social gathering showing boredom/confidence, defensive-ness, and cooperation/acceptance

slightly clenched together on their laps. These are very protective positions. From their secretive communication one might assume that they know each other very well and probably share many common interests. At the left is a seated young woman talking to a standing young man. The woman's head is tilted, her eyes are wide open, she is leaning forward slightly, and her arms are also open. The congruity of her gestures indicates that she is very interested in and receptive to what the young man is saying. He is preening himself with a tie-adjusting gesture as he leans down and forward toward the woman. He appears to be someone who is "putting his best foot forward"—as indeed he is, as indicated by the placement of his right foot. As Emerson said, "When man meets his fitting mate, society begins."

In Figure 73 the two men in the center are discussing something that has caused the man on the right to be defensive or uncomfortable. This is signaled by his crossed arms and legs. The other man has sensed his withdrawal and is attempting to open up their lines of communication by his gestures of open palms and widespread arms. He might almost be saying, "What's the matter? Did I say something wrong?" In this position he appears sincere in his request for feedback information that may not be forthcoming, judging from the facial expressions of downturned eyebrows, furrowed brow, grimace, and glaring eyes. Perhaps it is just as well that the hostile man will not express himself, otherwise there might be a torrent of angry words that would engulf all the others in the group. The two women seated on the right are very close friends and comfortable in each other's presence. Each has one leg tucked under her and is facing the other in an open position, obviously very much interested in the other's conversation. These two women would probably be the most surprised persons at the party if the two standing men were to start a vehement argument, since they have not bothered to look at them, much less observe the interaction. Notice also how each woman has an arm over the backrest of the couch, enabling them to almost touch each other if need be for reassurance or interrupt gestures. Their smiles are broad, showing teeth, and do not appear to be contrived. The woman seated on the left is not very attentive or interested in the young man standing in front of her. She has her legs crossed and is kicking her toe in the air in a steady cadence. Moreover, she has her arms crossed and is leaning away rather than toward the young man with her. The young man is very sure and smug about what he is saying but appears to be more concerned with himself than with the woman. He is steepling and has his nose in the air. The woman probably feels he is delivering a sermon or lecture to her rather than conversing. How much longer she puts up with this will depend on how patient she is or how observant he is of her reactions.

The two men in the center of Figure 74 are reacting to each other in a suspicious and nervous manner. The man on the right has silhouetted his body to the other man; his peering glance over the rims of his glasses and his hand thrust in his pocket suggest suspicion or doubt about what is being said. The man on the left is nervous and upset by what he has said and by the other man's reaction to it. He is trying to cover up something he has said by putting a hand over his mouth. The other hand is feeling the material of his coat in a reassurance gesture. The gesture of standing off balance with his legs crossed is congruous with his other gestures of nervousness. If we were to see this person five or ten seconds later, he might be rubbing his nose and shifting the weight of his body from foot to foot. Of the two seated women the one on the right has taken a very pronounced evaluative position to communicate her attitude to her companion, who seeks constantly, by holding out her hand and touching, a strong need for reassurance. Notice how the woman on the right is leaning away from her companion. In most situations where people get together,

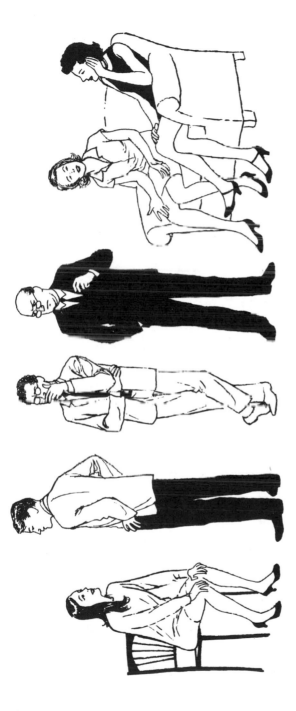

74. Social gathering showing readiness, nervousness/suspicion, and reassurance/evaluation

**75. Social gathering showing frustration/self-control**

there is at least one who is always attempting to sell an idea, service, or product, and someone else who is reluctantly cast in the buyer's role. The couple on the left is giving every indication of readiness, although it is impossible to read what they are ready for. They may be ready to dance or even to leave the party. Only a later set of gesture-clusters would reveal what action they contemplate. The young man with his hands on his hips is ready, willing, and able to carry out his plans for the evening, and the young woman, sensing this, responds by sitting on the edge of her chair, up on her toes, hands on her knees, and leaning forward like a sprinter ready for the starter's gun. If we were to observe each one more closely, we might see that the pupils of their eyes are dilated by what they see as very pleasing. This couple's interaction has resulted in the dynamics of activity that may lead to greater involvement.

The two men in Figure 75 are displaying very strong emotions. The one on the right is holding his arm behind his back in a gesture of self-control, and the person on the left is displaying a "beating" gesture based on frustration. This discus-

**76. The bore and his victim**
Did you ever get a feeling when sitting next to someone at a social function that he was very smug and would top anything you had to say? The above illustration may bring the situation to mind. With hands clasped behind his head and legs crossed in an American competitive position, the person on the left is telling his unhappy companion what great things he has done or is about to do. On the other hand, the person on the right is feeling that he has heard all of this before and would rather be somewhere else.

## 77. The suppressed gesture

The alert observer can notice the formation of a gesture and attempt to suppress it. Even the most guarded person can give himself away by the gestures he almost makes. The man on the left is such a person. He is being extremely cautious about what he is saying. Not only is his coat buttoned, but his left hand is encumbered with a glass and his free hand is hidden in his pocket. The listener on the right is basically open to what is being said and is ready for action. However, the man in the center is not accepting anything. The buttoned coat and hands in pockets are congruent with his facial expression, which indicates dislike or disbelief.

sion should be broken up immediately before the two come to blows. Many hosts and hostesses have unconsciously observed this cluster of gestures and take steps to remedy the situation. A bartender we interviewed remarked that when he saw two men arguing he always looked for the one rubbing the back of his neck. He usually threw the first punch.

**78. The audience nobody wants**
The speaker is leaning forward, actively trying to get his message across. How is it being received? Judging by the crossed arms, clasped hands, crossed legs, downturned lips, and furrowed brows, not at all well. Only the listener on the right shows a definite interest in what is being said, as indicated by his slightly tilted head, but his total reaction is negative. The speaker, aware of their indifference or hostility, clasps his hands apprehensively and may be about to wring them.

As a final test, without reading the captions on Figures 79–83, try to determine the nonverbal communication of each of the five girls whom you might see at a typical social gathering.

79. (Left) This girl is bored. The giveaway gestures are head in the palm of her hand and body pointing toward an exit.

80. (Right) This girl is striking an "I'm interested in you" pose. Hopefully the man is making preening gestures and is about to approach.

81. (Left) This woman is being very defensive, as indicated by her crossed arms and legs. If after a man has joined her she does not shift to a more open position, he might as well forget it.

82. (Right) The very feminine preening gesture of stroking her hair is congruent with her downcast eyes and presents a fine cluster of courting gestures. Note that her thumb is under her belt. Just as when a man uses it, the gesture means "everything is under control."

83. (Left) This woman is expecting someone—someone she is very fond of.

You are now on your own. Your life will be the laboratory. Your relationships will provide the experiments, and we hope our work has supplied you with sufficient procedures, equipment, and information for such work.

The sharing of any insights that you may have gained with your family, your friends, and your opposers will be most rewarding. Others have used this material to manipulate. We prefer that you view it on a larger scope. A person who is able to see only that he can gain a mechanical advantage by putting a long handle on a water pump sees only one application. A long pump handle not only provides a mechanical advantage but also permits two people to work together on the handle.

# Bibliography

ADLER, ALFRED. *Understanding Human Nature.* New York: Fawcett Premier Book, 1954.

ALLPORT, G. W., and VERNON, P. L. *Studies in Expressive Behavior.* New York: Hafner Publishing Company, 1933 and 1967.

ARDREY, ROBERT. *The Social Contract.* New York: Atheneum, 1970.

————. *The Territorial Imperative.* New York: Atheneum, 1966.

ARGYLE, MICHAEL. *The Psychology of Interpersonal Behavior.* Baltimore: Pelican Publications, 1967.

BACON, ALBERT M. *A Manual of Gestures.* Chicago: Silver Burdett Co., 1893.

BARNLUND, DEAN C., and HAIMAN, FRANKLYN S. *The Dynamics of Discussion.* Boston: Houghton Mifflin, 1960.

BERELSON, BERNARD, and STEINER, GARY A. *Human Behavior.* New York: Harcourt, Brace & World, Inc., 1964.

BERNE, ERIC. *Games People Play.* New York: Grove Press, Inc., 1964.

BIRDWHISTELL, RAY L. *Introduction to Kinesics.* Louisville, Ky.: University of Louisville Press, 1952.

————. *Kinesics and Context.* Philadelphia: University of Pennsylvania Press, 1970.

BRUNER, J. S., and GOODNOW, J. J. *A Study of Thinking.* New York: John Wiley, 1957.

CHAPMAN, A. H. *Put Offs and Come Ons.* New York: Putnam, 1968.

CHASE, STUART. *The Proper Study of Mankind.* New York: Harper, 1956.

CHERRY, C. *On Human Communication.* Cambridge, Mass.: M. I. T. Press, 1961.

CRITCHLEY, M. *The Language of Gesture.* London: Arnold, 1939.

DARWIN, CHARLES. *The Expression of Emotion in Man and Animals.* Chicago: The University of Chicago Press, 1965.

————. *The Origin of Species*. New York: Mentor Books, 1958.

DAVITZ, R. J. *The Communication of Emotional Meaning*. New York: McGraw-Hill, 1964.

DETHIER, V. G., and STELLAR, ELIOT. *Animal Behavior*. Englewood Cliffs, N.J. : Prentice-Hall, Inc., 1961.

EFRON, D. *Gesture and Environment*. New York: King's Crown, 1941.

ENNEIS, JAMES. *Everybody Does It*. Naval Aircraft Maintenance Management Course, 1965.

FAST, JULIUS. *Body Language*. Philadelphia: M. Evans and Co., Inc., 1970.

FELDMAN, SANDOR S. *Mannerisms of Speech and Gesture*. New York: International Universities Press, Inc., 1959.

FROMM, ERICH. *The Forgotten Language*. New York: Grove Press, Inc., 1951.

GOFFMAN, ERVING. *Behavior in Public Places*. New York: The Free Press, 1969.

————. *Interaction Ritual*. New York: Anchor Books, 1967.

————. *The Presentation of Self in Everyday Life*. New York: Anchor Books, 1959.

HALL, E. T. *Silent Language*. New York: Doubleday and Co., 1959.

————. *The Hidden Dimension*. New York: Doubleday and Co., 1966.

HALSMAN, PHILIPPE. *The Jump Book*. New York: Simon & Schuster, 1959.

HAYAKAWA, S. I. *Language in Thought and Action*. New York: Harcourt, Brace, 1949.

HAYES, FRANCIS. "Gestures, A Working Bibliography," *Southern Folklore Quarterly*, University of Florida, pp. 218–317, 1957. This article contains 910 references to books and articles on gestures, all of which have been evaluated.

JAMES, WILLIAM. *Principles of Psychology*. New York: Holt, Rinehart, 1892.

JOHNSON, WENDELL. *People in Quandaries*. New York: Harper, 1946.

JONES, HARRY. *Sign Language.* The English Universities Press Ltd., 1968.

JOURARD, SIDNEY M. *The Transparent Self.* New York: Van Nostrand, 1964.

JUNG, CARL G. *Man and His Symbols.* New York: Doubleday and Co., 1964.

KOCH, RUDOLF. *The Book of Signs.* London: First Edition Club, 1926.

KORZYBSKI, ALFRED. *Manhood of Humanity.* New York: E. P. Dutton, 1921.

———. *Science and Sanity.* The International Non-Aristotelian Library Publishing Company, 1958.

LAMB, WARREN. *Posture and Gesture.* Duckworth, 1965.

———, and TURNER, DAVID. *Management Behavior.* New York: International Universities Press, Inc., 1969.

LORENZ, KONRAD Z. *King Solomon's Ring.* New York: Crowell, 1952.

———, *On Aggression.* Harcourt, Brace & World, Inc., 1966.

MASLOW, A. H. *Motivation and Personality.* New York: Harper, 1954.

MILLER, G. H. *Language and Communication.* New York: McGraw-Hill, 1951.

MORRIS, CHARLES W. *Signs, Language and Behavior.* New York: George Braziller, Inc., 1955.

MORRIS, DESMOND. *The Human Zoo.* New York: McGraw-Hill, 1969.

———. *The Naked Ape.* New York: McGraw-Hill, 1967.

MORTON, D. J., and FULLER, D. D. *Human Locomotion and Body Form.* Baltimore: Williams and Wilkins, 1952.

MURRAY, ELWOOD. *The Speech Personality.* New York: Lippincott (revised edition), 1944.

NIERENBERG, GERARD I. *The Art of Negotiating.* New York: Hawthorn Books, Inc., 1968.

———. *Creative Business Negotiating.* New York: Hawthorn Books, Inc., 1971.

OGDEN, C. K., and RICHARD, I. A. *The Meaning of Meaning.* New York: Harcourt, Brace and Company, 1923, 1958.